The Magic of Broths

60 GREAT RECIPES FOR HEALING BROTHS AND STOCKS, AND HOW TO MAKE THEM

THE Magic OF Broths

60 GREAT RECIPES FOR HEALING BROTHS AND STOCKS, AND HOW TO MAKE THEM

Nick Sandler

Photography by Ali Allen Illustrations by Ruth Ferrier

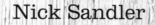

KYLE BOOKS

This book is dedicated to Lai, who manifests

First published in Great Britain in 2015 by
Kyle Books an imprint of Kyle Cathie Limited
192–198 Vauxhall Bridge Road
London SW1V 1DX
general.enquiries@kylebooks.com
www.kylebooks.com

10 9 8 7 6 5 4 3 2 1

ISBN 978 0 85783 346 4

A CIP catalogue record for this title is available from the British Library

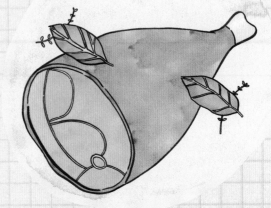

Editor: Kyle Cathie and Claire Rogers
Copy editor: Stephanie Evans
Design: Mark Latter, Blue Dragonfly Ltd
Food styling: Linda Tubby
Props styling: Ali Allen
Recipe analysis: Alina Tierney
Production: Gemma John, Nic Jones & Lisa Pinnell

Colour reproduction by ALTA London
Printed and bound in China by C&C Offset Printing Co., Ltd.

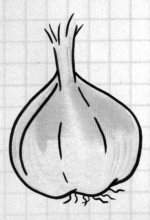

contents

broths

Don't think of broths as something boring and tasteless, simmering away in a tarnished stockpot, flavoured with a few old turnips and salty as hell. Today's are refined and delicious, spicy and aromatic, full-flavoured and satisfying. Broths can be made quickly and cheaply from bones, vegetables, herbs and spices and the recipes in this book are meals in their own right with the addition of rice, noodles, meat, seafood and pulses. Bone broths contain the essence of flavour and are the soul and spirit of the kitchen. Chicken and beef bones make great broth. Broths ensure the efficient use of ingredients from the fridge and reduce waste in the kitchen.

Broths are versatile

My wife is Chinese Malaysian. We have two kids, Jack and Amy, who, to be honest, prefer Far Eastern food to European - we get through a lot of broth! I always have a rich chicken and pork stock ready and waiting in the fridge. I just add a spoonful of ready prepared curry paste, rice noodles, fresh garden vegetables and, if I'm in the mood, a fillet or two of teriyaki mackerel. Our kids love their broths for breakfast, lunch and dinner. We lead busy lives and broths tick quite a few boxes for those of us who love food with delectable flavours, served on the hoof.

Broths are great for everyday eating, both at home and in a packed lunch, but are also delectable at dinner parties. My Mediterranean broth with clams is a great example of an easy yet exotic dish that will impress your friends.

Broths are healthy!

I eat broth every day but not every meal. I believe that broths can contribute to a balanced diet along with a good variety of fresh fruit and vegetables and a small amount of carbs and meat. They offer lots of punchy flavours to look forward to every day of the week, prepared with fine, fresh ingredients. Nutritionally broths are magic, being low salt, low fat and absolutely rammed with tonics derived from bones, vegetables and spices. You can broth yourself thin!

It's important for you to be aware of the nutritional content of your food so I've listed the calories, total fat, saturated fat, sugar and salt content of each dish.

Fresh revelations are made every day on the health benefits of bone broth. Of interest to both young and old alike are those nutrients that strengthen our skeletal systems, reducing swelling in joints from disease or injury. Bone broth can aid digestion, fight acid reflux and keep your gut in generally good order. And it seems that broths may help in detoxification. Add the benefits of bone marrow and a range of minerals, from calcium to magnesium, potassium to phosphorous, and the humble broth is elevated to elixir.

Celebrities are attributing their shiny golden locks and plump healthy skin to a diet of bone broths. But let's not get too carried away! Now you're going to have to spend a little time in the kitchen, fine tuning your own beautiful broth, the backbone of the delicious recipes in this book.

Where to get your bones

At the butcher's bones used to be a waste product but now they are kept locked up, never on display, for those discerning customers who really need them. When you ask your butcher for bones he may look you up and down and calculate a price based on the desperation etched upon your face, but my advice is to keep cool, buy a small cut of meat and as the transaction concludes casually ask if he has anything spare for the stockpot. There's money in old bones!

On the other hand, all the meat people at my local farmer's market sell bones, generally by the bag, and these are good organic bones, from people I know. If I ask in advance the beef man will slice the marrow bones so that they will fit in the pan and cook quicker.

Raw vs cooked bones

I roast my beef bones before simmering in the stockpot, but only occasionally roast my chicken bones. Beef bones love being caramelised in the oven – it brings out those gorgeous roast dinner flavours. Chicken bones make great stock unroasted and the light, meaty flavour adapts well to many recipes. There is very little nutritional difference between roasted and unroasted bones.

Stock-making, top tips

Making your own stock is therapeutic. There's something uplifting and unique about a delicious pot of homemade broth. Perhaps it is that depth of flavour, achieved without artificial powders, bouillons and MSG, or the fact that you've been watching the pot simmer all day and you're being driven mad by the aromas as the delicate herbs, earthy root vegetables and beautiful bones give up their goodness.

I feel empty when the stock has run out, so I always keep a little bit too much in the fridge and a pot or two in the freezer. Good stocks are kitchen currency.

A dollop buys you tasty steamed vegetables, a few tablespoons will improve gravies and sauces, a cup or two is the backbone of a ravishingly fresh and attractive broth to make a meal in itself. At the end of the week you can empty your leftovers – with a few provisos – into the stockpot. Stocks react badly to old, slimy vegetables; however a partially dehydrated mushroom improves the flavour. Some vegetables, such as leeks and brassicas, can skew the flavour balance of a good stock. Herbs, especially bay, sage and rosemary, are overpowering if you're heavy handed with them. So base your stocks around tried and tested recipes.

Stocks love being cooked slowly and gently, either on the hob or in the oven. Cooking at a gentle simmer for several hours results in sublime flavour extraction. My version of a gentle simmer is a steady stream of bubbles (maybe 5mm diameter) in one or two locations on the surface of the liquid.

Caress your stock, love it and the prize, translucent pots of golden set jelly (if making a bone broth), will be your friend in the fridge for the rest of the week.

- If you are concerned about leaving the stock simmering away as you run a few errands you can always turn the heat off and switch it back on when you return. My stockpot sits nicely over the smallest gas ring, keeping it just below boiling point. I find that if I get the temperature right only a small amount of evaporation occurs over the cooking process.

- Chefs order us to skim the fat off our stocks, but I never do this. I let the fat rest on the surface as it slowly simmers away. It's a fallacy that doing so leads to a fattier stock, as long as you simmer, not boil. The action of a rolling boil dissolves the fat into the liquid, which is why you need to keep your stock bubbling but not boiling.

- I decant the stock, fat and all, after cooking through a large sieve into a voluminous bowl. I dip my trusty jug into the dangerously hot liquid and carefully pour into small Tupperware pots with tight-fitting lids. Once the lid is on, be careful. The stock is still giving off a lot of steam and a little shake may dislodge the lid with a pop!

- When you strain your stocks make sure you squeeze every drop of goodness from the ingredients by pressing down with the back of a spoon.

- Cool your stock down as quickly as you can. Winter is a good time for this. On a frosty or snowy day you can merely leave the containers outside for a couple of hours and the work is done, otherwise you can do the following:

  - Place the pots of stock in a large bowl of cold water – or use the sink. The water should come up to just below the lids. Refresh the cold water every 10 minutes and the stock will be at room temperature within 30 minutes or so. If you add ice to the water it speeds up the process.

  - Let the stock cool in your kitchen. This may take a couple of hours and if you opt for this slightly longer cooling process I would reduce the stock's shelf life in your fridge to 5 days, otherwise it will last for 7 days.

Useful items of broth-making equipment

I simmer my stocks in stainless steel saucepans and usually make large batches, especially of beef stock as it takes so long to make. Ten litre saucepans are perfect. Long handled lifters and skimmers are useful for attending to your stocks as they cook. Conical sieves work well for fish and veggie stocks as you can squeeze every ounce of liquid goodness through them with the back of a large spoon. Any other large strainer works well for filtering chicken and beef stock.

Plastic, ceramic or glass containers with tight fitting lids store your stocks safely in the fridge and if I have the choice I use those of a smaller capacity – around 500ml. Ice-cube trays are made for freezing small amounts of concentrated stock. Once frozen the cubes should be stored in a freezer bag.

Marrow Bone Wars

It's important to choose good bones for your stocks, ideally from organic farms. When you boil a bone, nutrients and minerals are dissolved into the liquid so any drugs, such as antibiotics, that are ingested by the animals will be present as well; in greater and greater concentrations as the stock boils down. Organic animals are farmed on organic land. Such land is tested to make sure that it is free from banned pesticides, fungicides and heavy metals such as cadmium, mercury and lead.

If you are not sure about the provenance of the bones just ask. This is easy at the farmers' market and it's also becoming easier to ask the supermarkets, just tweet them and they'll answer quick, believe me!

Until recently bones went in the bin. Now everybody wants them, especially when the bones have come from a good organic farm. Recently my wife had a run-in with another woman over marrow bone at the farmers' market. The bones had been pre-ordered by us but the contender had spotted them and wanted the prize. According to Ray the fish man there was an intense standoff, followed by martial arts, of the highest order. My wife won, but I told her not to return to the market for a few weeks.

Broth Diets

Broths taste delicious and are indispensable in my kitchen, but I do have private thoughts... What if broths serve another purpose, what if they're good for you? I mean, doughnuts taste great, but nobody's making any health claims for them.

Broths are indulgent but many are claiming a functionality that goes far beyond the simple pleasures. I resolved to find out whether it's possible to flourish on a broth diet and to measure the results in a subjective sort of way. Maybe this is my opportunity to forget the powders and pills, to emancipate myself from flaxseed, powdered hemp and chia, because, let's face it, they taste of nothing and could be anything! But now for the scientific bit...

Bone Broth Nutrition

The fundamental ingredient of most of my broths is bones, which are made up of protein (mainly collagen) and minerals. Bones are also a good source of fat. Even the Neanderthals used all kinds of procedures to extract the fat contained in bone tissue. And when we learned how to wet-cook, i.e. 'boil', we realised that we could greatly increase the digestibility and nutritional worth of foods, including bones.

To get the goodness from the bone, extensive cooking times are required (up to 12 hours). The longer the cooking time, the more porous the bone becomes allowing the proteins, fat and, to some extent, minerals to leach into the boiling water and thus enrich the broth with all the good nutrients.

Historically, people have realised that broths not only offer a means of meeting nutritional needs but also benefit health. Your mother was right when she fed you chicken soup when you were run down; it has been proven to contain compounds of potential medical value, which help you recover faster from a cold. Anecdotally, bone broths have been used for ailments that affect the joints, skin and gastrointestinal tract due to its collagen content, and for bone health as they contain calcium and magnesium, two minerals important for bone formation.

Alina Tierney, nutritionist and fellow climber, proposed that my broths would make good choices for people who follow intermittent fasting diets, calorie restriction diets, or diets that are based on bone broths, such as the Gut and Psychology Syndrome (GAPS) diet, which addresses neurological disorders through dietary change.

Despite being practised for millennia in many cultures for both health and religious reasons, fasting diets have only recently received the attention of the scientific community. There is no common consensus on the definition of fasting, but generally it means eating or drinking between 0 and 30 percent of your normal daily calorie intake. Intermittent fasting, for example where you fast for 2 days a week and have a normal calorie intake on the other 5 days, proposes 600 kcal for a man and 500 kcal for a woman on the 2 fasting days.

Fasting has been shown to not only help lose weight but also to offer a wide array of other health benefits, such as improvements in blood pressure and cholesterol levels, protection against diabetes and even rebooting the immune system by clearing out the immune cells and regenerating new ones, which could help reduce the ageing process. Scientists have also found that both blood glucose and inflammation have been reduced in people that follow this style of diet, as the body is tricked into thinking that it's being starved. It has also been shown to enhance brain function and promote the growth of beneficial bacteria in the gut. So many benefits that it is worth a try!

Diet experiments

I did two diet experiments, each one lasting five days, with the aim of measuring the effects of a broth diet on my mind and body. These diets need a little planning, as you'll need to make the stocks in advance, but once the pots of goodness are installed in the fridge the rest is simple.

For the first experiment, I wanted to follow a meal plan that did not leave me feeling empty, unfulfilled or discontented. I ate broth for every meal but if I was hungry or fancied something else I would have it. For example, this is what I had on the first day:

Breakfast: sesame omelette and pork broth
Mid-morning snack: veggie smoothie
Lunch: pork fritters in broth with tomatoes and sliced onions
Mid-afternoon snack: handful of nuts mid-afternoon
Dinner: light Caldo Verde broth

After 5 days, I compared, before and after, weight, strength, healing, digestion and sheer man beauty – not including hair growth as it's too late!

Weight – no change.
Strength – I am a climber and after the diet I was able to make serious attempts on climbs two grades above my previous level. Of course, this may have been a placebo effect but I was absolutely delighted!
Healing – my sports injuries are generally painful but since the diet they have been less acute.
Digestion – I do occasionally suffer from indigestion, probably due to a high fat diet, but the diet seemed to alter the acid balance in my stomach and I haven't suffered since.
Beauty – I asked a number of people whether they'd noticed a difference in my skin tone and whether they found me increasingly

attractive, handsome or just awesomely hot! This was the most disappointing area of research. There was no change here, just slightly perplexed looks. My wife told me that a little housework might make me more handsome.

For the second experiment I had only broths for the main meals with nothing else in between. I assumed that this would reduce my calorie intake and therefore lead to losing some weight.

According to Alina, any of the broth recipes would be good for following a calorie restriction diet as long as the starchy ingredients such as noodles, potatoes and rice are omitted (see page 12). Here is what a fasting day would look like:

Breakfast: sesame omelette and pork broth, using 1 egg and without the rice noodles (260 kcal per 400g serving)
Lunch: harira with saffron and freekeh (179 kcal per 300g serving)
Dinner: spiced beef tea (82 kcal per 1 cup)

This second experiment resulted in a 2.5% loss of my body weight and the benefits that I saw with the first experiment continued.

Carbs and their Calorific Impact

Weight for weight, carbohydrate has half the calories of fat, so should you be worried about carbs if you watch your weight? The answer is yes.

We don't have the ability to store carbohydrates – any excess not used for energy is converted to fat and stored in the adipose tissue (connective tissue found around your internal organs, bone marrow and muscles). If you don't use up the energy you eat, it accumulates as fat around your waist and thighs.

Carbohydrates come from plant and fruit sources. The ones that you need to watch out for are carbohydrates that are broken down more easily into simple sugars, as these lead to increased glucose in the bloodstream, which triggers the release of insulin. Insulin tells the cells to convert these simple sugars into either energy or fat but if you have too much it results in more fat. So, by keeping your carbohydrate intake low you keep the insulin levels low and so store less fat.

Fat has more than double the calories of carbohydrates; so doesn't eating fat lead to more weight gain? In fact, fat metabolism requires almost no insulin and it slows down the glucose release into the bloodstream, which in turn reduces insulin release. Fat also makes you feel full quicker, so you will most likely eat less food.

So, it is not so much the calorie intake that is important, but where the calories come from and the impact of their sources on fat metabolism.

Most of the carbohydrates in this book are complex carbohydrates, which have a lesser effect on insulin levels. Nevertheless, I have listed opposite the foods that are high in carbohydrates and their calorific content per 50g increments, so that you can either have less or leave them out of the recipe if you follow a low-carb diet or want to watch your weight.

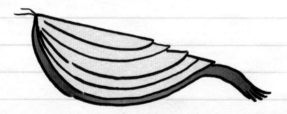

Carb table

	Kcal per 50g	Kcal per 100g	Kcal per 150g
Polenta, cornmeal, dry	184	368	552
Polenta, baked or boiled	43	85	170
Haricot beans, cooked	40	79	119
Rice noodles, cooked	55	109	165
Ramen noodles, cooked	69	138	207
Potatoes, boiled	36	72	108
White rice, boiled	62	124	186
Brown rice, boiled	70	141	212
Quinoa, cooked	60	120	180
Cannellini beans, cooked	48	95	142
Fettuccine	80	159	238
Sweetcorn, kernel, boiled in unsalted water	56	111	166
Freekeh wheat, dry	162	325	488
Chickpeas, whole, boiled	60	121	182
Chestnuts	85	170	255
Matzos	192	384	576
Soba Japanese noodles, cooked	50	99	149
Breadcrumbs	177	354	531

Beef

Beef broth is the motherlode, the magic bullet, the recently discovered golden elixir that's been around for millennia.

Our grandmothers instinctively knew that beef broth possessed life-boosting properties. Florence Nightingale existed on it for the last few years of her life. Dissolved within it is a cornucopia of minerals and amino acids that are readily absorbed by the body.

Beef broths have a growing fan base and, let's face it, any potion that keeps you healthy, makes you live longer and tastes great gets my total approval.

Marrow bones cut into sections or in half lengthways are perfect for beef stock. I also use oxtail, meat included, as it's easy to obtain.

beef stock

Much of the flavour in this stock is derived from the roasting of the bones. All the ingredients are available in butchers and supermarkets, although you may need to order the marrow bones in advance. Even though the total cooking time – 12 hours – for this timeless classic is lengthy, the actual preparation time is minimal, leaving you free to get on with your day. I get my stock going first thing in the morning and decant off the broth last thing at night so that I don't have to fret about it boiling away as I sleep. The main thing is not to worry about it: it is what it is. Beef broth is not fussy, just a jumble of meat and vegetables giving up their goodness for you. And whenever my friends ask me what the secret of a good stock is, I tell them that simmering is good, boiling is bad. Patience is paramount!

You will need 2 large baking trays and an extra-large saucepan – at least 10-litre capacity.

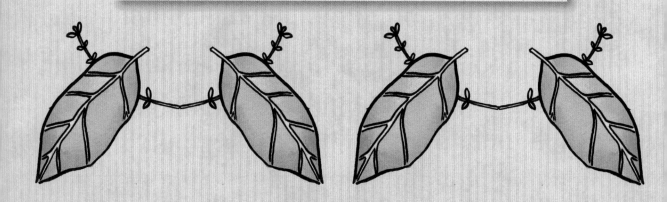

Preheat the oven to 220°C/200° fan/gas mark 7.

Put the beef marrow bones, beef scraps, oxtail, shallots and garlic on the baking trays and bake for 1 hour, until caramelised and brown.

Transfer the baked ingredients to the saucepan and top with the rest of the ingredients. Fill with enough water to just cover the ingredients.

Bring just to the boil and simmer for 12 hours over a very low heat. Keep a watchful eye on the stock as it simmers. As the liquid evaporates the stock will increase in temperature – you want to keep it gently bubbling and not boiling.

Decant through a large strainer into a voluminous bowl or saucepan and then further decant into airtight containers. Chill in a sink half filled with cold water to take the edge off the heat and, once at room temperature, place in the fridge where it will store for up to a week.

makes 1 litre

PER 100G 33 KCALS, PROTEIN 4.4G, CARBS 0.6G,
FAT 1.4G, SAT FAT 0.5G, FIBRE 0.3G, SUGAR 0.5G, SALT TRACE

3KG BEEF MARROW BONES, CUT INTO SECTIONS
    OR IN HALF LENGTHWAYS
1KG BEEF SCRAPS FROM LEAN MEAT
1KG OXTAIL, CUT INTO SECTIONS
500G SHALLOTS, TRIMMED AND CUT IN HALF
1 LARGE HEAD OF GARLIC, CUT IN HALF
1 MEDIUM LEEK, WASHED AND CUT IN HALF
4 CELERY STICKS, WASHED AND BROKEN IN TWO
5 MEDIUM CARROTS, DIRT REMOVED, CHUNKY CUT
1 MEDIUM TURNIP, SLICED
A SMALL BUNCH OF FLAT-LEAF PARSLEY
2 BAY LEAVES
A HANDFUL OF THYME
100G TOMATO PURÉE
2 TABLESPOONS WHITE WINE VINEGAR
1 LEVEL TABLESPOON (5G) PORCINI MUSHROOM
    POWDER (OPTIONAL)
2 TABLESPOONS WHITE WINE VINEGAR

Simmered slices of beetroot and new potato served in a tangy beef broth with oxtail is totally delicious. This brightly coloured broth is an absolute culinary revelation and shows us why traditional Polish or Russian borscht should always be cooked with freshly made beef stock. And it won't take you more than half an hour. This is a great recipe to make in the following days after you've made beef stock as it uses meat from the oxtail, one of the principal ingredients.

simple beef borscht

Dry-fry the aniseed and coriander seed in a pan over a moderate heat for a couple of minutes until they start to brown and the aromas fill the kitchen. Crush using a pestle and mortar.

Add the beef stock to a medium saucepan along with the potatoes, beetroot, spices, brandy, cherry tomatoes, white wine vinegar and porcini powder. Simmer for 20 minutes until the potato and beetroot are cooked, add the meat and season with salt and pepper.

Serve in bowls topped with sprigs of dill and soured cream.

serves 4

PER SERVING 298 KCALS, PROTEIN 25.9G, CARBS 19.8G, FAT 10.7G, SAT FAT 4.3G, FIBRE 3.2G, SUGAR 8.8G, SALT 1.7G

½ TEASPOON ANISEED
½ TEASPOON CORIANDER SEEDS
750ML BEEF STOCK (SEE PAGE 17)
300G NEW POTATOES, WASHED AND SLICED
200G RAW BEETROOT, WASHED AND SLICED
30ML BRANDY
100G CHERRY TOMATOES, SLICED
20ML WHITE WINE VINEGAR
1 TEASPOON PORCINI MUSHROOM POWDER
300G OXTAIL MEAT, REMOVED FROM THE BONE
    AND CUT INTO LARGE PIECES, DISCARDING
    ANY CARTILAGE OR SINEW
SALT AND FRESHLY GROUND BLACK PEPPER

TO SERVE
FRESH DILL
SOURED CREAM (OPTIONAL)

Pho is a broth that encapsulates the recent history of a nation, flavoured with local spices, influenced by French cuisine and eaten by US pilots. Pho is slow-cooked beef stock infused with spices and served with sliced beef, crunchy vegetables and scented herbs.

Pho has its origins in 1920s Vietnam, where felt-hatted vendors touted this homemade delicacy for breakfast and dinner on two long poles, one for broth and the other for garnishes and spices. Today's pho follows the same principles: the beef stock comes first. The masterful broth maker keeps the exact recipe locked away, but I'm terrible at keeping secrets so read mine and I'll reveal all.

pho

Preheat the oven to 220°C/200° fan/gas mark 7.

Place the shallots, garlic and ginger on a medium baking tray, sprinkle with 2 tablespoons of the vegetable oil and loosely toss to coat. Bake in the oven for 30 minutes, until golden brown.

Meanwhile, dry-fry the fennel and coriander seeds in a pan over a low heat for 5 minutes or until they start to darken and are persuasively aromatic. Remove from the heat. Bundle up the fennel and coriander seeds, star anise, cloves, cardamom pods and cinnamon stick in a cheesecloth/muslin bag tied up with string.

Pour the beef stock into a large saucepan and add the aromatics, then add the shallots, garlic and ginger, leaving any excess oil on the baking tray. Add 1 tablespoon of the fish sauce and sugar. Simmer for 1 hour, perhaps topping up a little if more than 20 per cent of the liquid evaporates.

Meanwhile, season the steak with the remaining fish sauce and the paprika and coat with vegetable oil. Heat a frying pan and fry the steak over medium heat for 3 minutes on each side for medium. Slice thinly.

Add the rice noodles to the beef stock, briefly bring to the boil and then remove from heat. Ladle into bowls and top each one with the beef, beansprouts, herbs and red chilli. The lime juice is squeezed on last.

serves 4

PER SERVING 404 KCALS, PROTEIN 47.5G, CARBS 20.1G, FAT 14.1G, SAT FAT 4.2G, FIBRE 3.8G, SUGAR 6.2G, SALT 0.5G

FOR THE BROTH

1.2 LITRES BEEF STOCK (SEE PAGE 17)
8 MEDIUM SHALLOTS, PEELED, TRIMMED AND HALVED
4 CLOVES GARLIC, PEELED
15G FRESH GINGER ROOT, PEELED AND ROUGHLY
   SLICED
VEGETABLE OIL
½ TEASPOON FENNEL SEEDS
½ TEASPOON CORIANDER SEEDS
3 WHOLE STAR ANISE
4 CLOVES
2 CARDAMOM PODS
1 CINNAMON STICK
1½ TABLESPOONS FISH SAUCE
1–2 TEASPOONS SUGAR (OPTIONAL)
1 LARGE RUMP STEAK, APPROX. 400G
1 TEASPOON PAPRIKA
400G COOKED FLAT RICE NOODLES

TO FINISH

200G BEANSPROUTS
A SMALL BUNCH OF THAI BASIL, LEAVES PLUCKED
A SMALL BUNCH OF CORIANDER, MOST OF THE
   STALKS REMOVED
1 RED CHILLI, SLICED
2 LIMES, CUT INTO WEDGES

Please don't make this regularly; it is so disgracefully delicious it is probably very bad for you! The toasties are based on an ancient Finnish recipe, presumably one intended to keep out the winter cold. I've used Cheddar here as Finnish cheese is difficult to get hold of.

beef broth and marrow
with finnish toasties

Preheat the oven to 220°C/200° fan/gas mark 7.

Season the marrow bones, place on a baking tray marrow side up and bake in the oven for 40 minutes. Scoop out the marrow and discard the bones.

Mix the soured cream, almonds, Cheddar, nutmeg and salt and pepper in a small bowl to form a textured paste.

Spread the sourdough with butter. Turn two slices over so that the buttered sides are face down. Spread with the soured cream mix and top with the remaining two slices, buttered side up.

Heat a large frying pan and gently fry the Finnish toasties for 10 minutes on each side until golden brown and melting in the middle.

Meanwhile heat the beef stock and spoon in the bone marrow. Add salt and pepper and a pinch of chopped parsley if you like.

Cut the Finnish toasties into fingers and you're ready for some of the best dipping action you'll ever get!

serves 4

PER SERVING 807 KCALS, PROTEIN 36.3G, CARBS 77.2G, FAT 38G, SAT FAT 15.8G, FIBRE 5.2G, SUGAR 7.2G, SALT 5.6G

2 LONG MARROW BONES, HALVED LENGTHWAYS. (YOU CAN BUY THEM PREPARED IN THIS WAY FROM THE BUTCHER)
400ML BEEF STOCK (SEE PAGE 17)
CHOPPED FLAT-LEAF PARSLEY (OPTIONAL)
SALT AND FRESHLY GROUND BLACK PEPPER

FOR THE TOASTIES
2 HEAPED TABLESPOONS SOURED CREAM
2 HEAPED TABLESPOONS GROUND ALMONDS
2 HEAPED TABLESPOONS GRATED MATURE CHEDDAR
A PINCH OF GROUND NUTMEG
4 SLICES SOURDOUGH BREAD
BUTTER

Adelina Patti was one of the most famous sopranos in history. Born in 1843 she died in 1919. Towards the end of her life she made a number of recordings. Patti's legacy includes songs and arias from *Le Nozze di Figaro*, *Don Giovanni* and *Faust*. Her favourite snack was a rich beef broth with thinly sliced omelette and chestnuts, served to her before every performance. Maybe this is why her voice sounds so full and rich in her remastered recordings.

beef broth with chestnuts

Heat the beef stock in a medium saucepan and add the chestnuts.

Lightly whisk the eggs with spring onion and a touch of salt and pepper.

Heat the butter or olive oil in a large non-stick frying pan and pour in the omelette mix. Tilt the pan for maximum coverage and do not stir. Cook over a medium heat for a couple of minutes.

Turn out onto a chopping board and cut into thin strips before scraping the lot into the broth.

Serve in small bowls before a good karaoke session.

serves 2

PER SERVING 358 KCALS, PROTEIN 17.8G, CARBS 36.4G, FAT 14.2G, SAT FAT 3.6G, FIBRE 6.4G, SUGAR 8G, SALT 2.8G

400ML BEEF STOCK (SEE PAGE 17), SEASONED WITH
    SALT AND A PINCH OF WHITE PEPPER
20 COOKED AND PEELED CHESTNUTS, THINLY
    SLICED
2 LARGE EGGS
3 SPRING ONIONS, THINLY SLICED
SALT AND WHITE PEPPER
A KNOB OF BUTTER OR A COUPLE OF TEASPOONS
    OF OLIVE OIL

Beef brisket is made for slow roasting. It is beautifully textured and shreds to perfection. The beef can be roasted in advance and the rest is easy, I reckon 10 minutes maximum preparation time for a highly nutritious, delicious meal.

I've suggested using a handy pack of pre-cooked grains in this recipe. They're easy to find in the supermarket, either tinned or in those floppy plastic pyramid packs, thus saving you the bother of having to weigh out, boil and wait. The mix I use includes bulgur wheat, red lentils, red quinoa and soya. But use any grain you fancy.

beef brisket, grains and chard

Preheat the oven to 150°C/fan 130°C/gas mark 2.

Put the beef along with the stock, bay leaf, thyme, garlic and seasoning in a deep-sided oven dish, cover and bake for 3–4 hours. Check after a couple of hours to make sure the broth hasn't evaporated and top up with water if needed.

Remove from the oven and allow to cool for 30 minutes before shredding the brisket either with fingers or forks. Make sure you don't waste the gooey concentrated broth in the bottom of the pan. The beef can be roasted and shredded in advance and kept in the fridge for 3–4 days in an airtight container.

Heat the broth in a large saucepan and add the grains, chard, radishes, shredded beef and vinegar. Simmer briefly and serve immediately.

serves 4

PER SERVING 444 KCALS, PROTEIN 51.6G, CARBS 26G, FAT 14.8G, SAT FAT 5.7G, FIBRE 1.1G, SUGAR 1.8G, SALT 1.8G

FOR THE BEEF
750G BEEF BRISKET
200ML BEEF STOCK (SEE PAGE 17)
1 BAY LEAF
A FEW SPRIGS OF THYME
4 CLOVES GARLIC, PEELED AND CUT IN HALF
SALT AND FRESHLY GROUND BLACK PEPPER

FOR THE BROTH
800ML BEEF STOCK (SEE PAGE 17)
400G PRE-COOKED MIXED GRAINS
200G MIXED SWISS CHARD, SLICED
8 RADISHES, THINLY SLICED
1 TABLESPOON RED WINE OR SHERRY VINEGAR

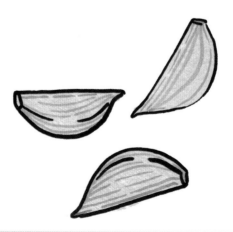

I often cook my beef over the weekend, when I've got time on my hands. Once shredded it keeps for a few days in the fridge. The final instructions for this recipe are incredibly simple so you'll have your meal on the table in no time.

chinese noodle hotpot
with beef, edamame and star anise

Preheat the oven to 120°C/100°C fan/gas mark ½.

Place the beef stock, beef brisket, star anise, ginger, honey, soy sauce, garlic, chilli and rice wine in a deep, lidded casserole dish. Cover and bake in the oven until the beef is meltingly good, approximately 4 hours.

Strain off the stock – but not into the sink and down the plughole (as I, foolishly, have done on occasion). Reserve the stock in a saucepan while the beef cools and then shred the beef with a couple of forks. If you wish you can store the stock and beef in the fridge for up to 4 days in airtight containers.

To finish the dish, reheat the stock with the beef. Once simmering, add the beans and season with a little dark soy sauce if you like.

Serve with piles of noodles.

serves 4

PER SERVING 513 KCALS, PROTEIN 59.4G, CARBS 24.6G, FAT 18.5G, SAT FAT 6.2G, FIBRE 5.4G, SUGAR 6.1G, SALT 1.1G

1.5 LITRES BEEF STOCK (SEE PAGE 17)
750G BEEF BRISKET
4 STAR ANISE
3CM PIECE (APPROX. 25G) OF FRESH GINGER ROOT, ROUGHLY SLICED
2 TEASPOONS HONEY
1 TABLESPOON DARK SOY SAUCE, PLUS EXTRA FOR SERVING
3 CLOVES GARLIC, PEELED
1 RED CHILLI
2 TABLESPOONS RICE WINE OR SHERRY
300G FROZEN EDAMAME BEANS (SOYA BEANS)
RAMEN NOODLES OR RICE NOODLES, TO SERVE (SEE PAGE 13)

A truly magical infusion featuring cardamom, cloves, star anise and crushed fennel seeds. This tonic has a floral aroma and layers of rich, complex flavour – it is truly the beef motherlode.

nick's spiced beef tea

Put the beef stock into a saucepan along with the star anise, cloves and ginger.

Lightly crush the fennel, cardamom and nutmeg using a pestle and mortar. Add to the saucepan. Bring to the boil then remove from the heat and let it sit for 10 minutes for the flavours to infuse.

Return to the heat, bring to the boil and strain off into cups through a fine strainer.

makes 2 medium cups

PER SERVING 82 KCALS, PROTEIN 9.5G, CARBS 2.3G, FAT 3.8G, SAT FAT 1.4G, FIBRE 0.6G, SUGAR 1.3G, SALT 0.1G

400ML BEEF STOCK (SEE PAGE 17)
1 STAR ANISE
4 CLOVES
3CM PIECE (APPROX. 25G) OF FRESH GINGER ROOT, SLICED – MAKE SURE IT'S CLEAN, BUT IT DOESN'T NEED TO BE PEELED
½ TEASPOON FENNEL SEEDS
3 CARDAMOM PODS
¼ NUTMEG

I came across an alluring mix of dried pulses in the supermarket. It contained yellow split peas, green split peas, marrowfat peas, barley, red lentils and adzuki beans. I decided to brazenly spice up beef stock with Worcestershire sauce and tomatoes and, with the word 'marrowfat' whizzing round my brain, emptied out a marrowbone and revived a recipe for amourettes, a bone marrow fritter popular in France during the nineteenth century.

pea and barley beef broth
with deliciously decadent amourettes

Put the beef stock in a large saucepan with the cooked pulse mix, Worcestershire sauce, cherry tomatoes and spring greens. Bring to the boil and cook for 5-8 minutes.

Meanwhile, using your fingers, mix the marrow with 40g of the breadcrumbs, the egg yolk and flat-leaf parsley in a medium sized bowl. It's fine to leave the marrow a bit chunky – don't let it get too warm or it will become sticky.

Roll out into a sausage and divide into eight sections. Press each bone marrow fritter into the remaining breadcrumbs.

Dry-heat a medium sized frying pan and gently fry the amourettes over a low heat for 4 minutes on each side until golden brown. (You don't have to add any oil to the pan as the amourettes will give off their own fat.)

Ladle the broth into bowls and top each portion with a couple of amourettes.

serves 4

PER SERVING 250 KCALS, PROTEIN 17.1G, CARBS 28.3G, FAT 6.8G, SAT FAT 2.3G, FIBRE 3.7G, SUGAR 3.7G, SALT 0.5G

600ML BEEF STOCK (SEE PAGE 17)

250G COOKED PULSE MIX (I USED THE ONE MENTIONED ABOVE BUT THERE ARE MANY GRAIN AND PULSE MIXES - JUST FOLLOW THE INSTRUCTIONS ON THE PACKET. FOR 250G COOKED PULSES YOU'LL NEED APPROX. 100G DRY MIX)

1 TABLESPOON WORCESTERSHIRE SAUCE

150G CHERRY TOMATOES, SLICED

100G SPRING GREENS, SHREDDED

100G BEEF MARROW SCOOPED FROM 2 MARROW BONES USING A TEASPOON

60G FRESH BREADCRUMBS (SAY 3 SLICES OF SOURDOUGH PULSED IN A FOOD PROCESSOR UNTIL ROUGHLY BLENDED. THE BETTER THE BREAD THE FIRMER THE TEXTURE OF THE BREADCRUMBS)

1 EGG YOLK

A SCRUNCHED-UP HANDFUL OF FLAT-LEAF PARSLEY, ROUGHLY CHOPPED

This is a sneaky version of the French classic. The original recipe requires a long and slow cook. I reckon you can get this one all wrapped up in about 45 minutes as your sumptuous beef broth, the base for this recipe, is ready and waiting in the fridge.

quick beef bourguignonne

Preheat the oven to 220°C/200° fan/gas mark 7.

Season the steaks with salt and freshly ground black pepper and rub with 1 tablespoon of olive oil. Set aside.

Pour the stock into a medium saucepan and add the wine, tomato purée, bay leaves and thyme. Bring to the boil and then reduce (that means let it boil away merrily) until about half the liquid has evaporated, over a medium heat. This should take 20–30 minutes.

Meanwhile, put the new potatoes, turnips, shallots and carrots on a baking tray, cover with a few glugs of olive oil and a sprinkling of salt, turn to make sure the vegetables are well coated in a thin layer of oil and bake in the oven for 30 minutes.

Add the vegetables to the broth leaving any excess oil on the baking tray. Put back on the heat for a minute to let all the flavours come together.

Meanwhile, heat a medium frying pan and fry the sirloins for 2 minutes on each side for rare or 3 minutes on each side for medium. Allow to cool slightly and thinly slice.

Season the chunky broth and serve in bowls. Top with the sliced sirloin divided into the 4 bowls.

serves 4

PER SERVING 445 KCALS, PROTEIN 39.6G, CARBS 31.3G, FAT 13.9G, SAT FAT 4.7G, FIBRE 7.8G, SUGAR 12.9G, SALT 3G

2 SIRLOIN STEAKS WEIGHING APPROX. 500G (250G EACH)
OLIVE OIL
1 LITRE BEEF STOCK (SEE PAGE 17)
250ML RED WINE
80G TOMATO PURÉE
2 BAY LEAVES
2 SPRIGS OF THYME
500G NEW POTATOES, WASHED AND CUT INTO 3CM CHUNKS
150G TURNIPS, WASHED AND CUT INTO 3CM CHUNKS
300G LONG SHALLOTS, PEELED AND SLICED INTO 3 PIECES
300G BABY CARROTS, WASHED AND TRIMMED, ROUGHLY SLICED, IF YOU LIKE
SALT AND FRESHLY GROUND BLACK PEPPER

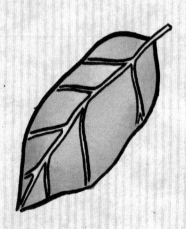

Pork

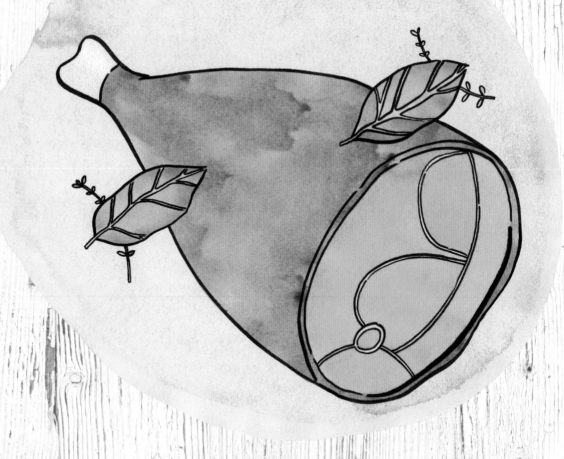

Have you ever wondered where all the pig's trotters go? To tell you the truth I hadn't either until a friend (who works for the UK's largest pork producer) told me that they go to China. They use them to make broth – lots of it. I use pig's trotters in my pork rib stock and chicken stock. In the fridge the stocks set into a firm jelly and are incredibly versatile as recipe ingredients. I propose that we take the trotters back from China and use them ourselves!

Pork is the unsung hero of the broth world, introducing a deep flavour to the stockpot. Pork bones boost Far Eastern dishes and adapt beautifully to European classics such as choucroûte and cassoulet. If you can buy organic so much the better; it's worth paying a little extra for flavour and provenance.

Pig's trotters contain collagen, the stuff that makes your skin plump and sexy. Collagen is available in lotions, drinks and pills, which don't taste very nice and are rather expensive, but let me suggest and alternative. For a nominal sum you can enjoy hearty food with friends and get your daily dose of collagen into the bargain!

With its delectable aroma and sensuous spice, this stock is perfect as a base for Asian noodle and rice dishes. I use my own home-dried, smoked chilli. You could use hot *pimentón de la Vera* or unsmoked chilli flake, but many versions are rather hot, so watch out!

pork rib stock

Place all the ingredients in a large saucepan with enough water to cover everything and bring to the boil. Reduce the heat to a gentle simmer. You don't want the liquid to bubble away merrily as it will reduce too fast and the surface oil will mix with the stock, making it taste fatty.

Simmer for most of the day, minimum 4 hours, preferably for 6–8 hours. You don't want to reduce the stock that much; maybe up to 5cm but not much more. If you notice the stock getting low, top up the level with water.

When the stock is ready the liquid will be clear and the meat melting off the bones. Decant through a large strainer into a voluminous bowl or saucepan and then further decant into airtight containers. Chill in a sink half filled with cold water to take the edge off the heat and, once at room temperature, place in the fridge where it will store for up to a week.

makes 1.8 litres
PER 100G
(WITH TROTTERS) 102 KCALS, PROTEIN 8.6G, CARBS 1.3G, FAT 7G, SAT FAT 1.6G, FIBRE 0.1G, SUGAR 0.2G, SALT 0.6G
(WITHOUT TROTTERS) 77 KCALS, PROTEIN 7G, CARBS 1.5G, FAT 4.8G, SAT FAT 1.8G, FIBRE 0.1G, SUGAR 0.2G, SALT 0.1G

2KG PORK RIBS, APPROX. 2 RACKS
1 PIG'S TROTTER (OPTIONAL)
100G FRESH SHIITAKE MUSHROOMS – DON'T WORRY ABOUT TRIMMING OR SLICING THEM
1 MEDIUM HEAD OF GARLIC, CUT IN HALF
30G TOMATO PASTE
80G FRESH GINGER ROOT, THICKLY SLICED (PROVIDED IT'S CLEAN IT DOESN'T NEED TO BE PEELED)
4 WHOLE STAR ANISE
6 CARDAMOM PODS
1 TEASPOON FENNEL SEEDS
½ NUTMEG, GRATED
1 TEASPOON RED CHILLI FLAKES
1 TEASPOON DRIED PORCINI MUSHROOM, SLICED OR POWDERED
25ML RICE VINEGAR
APPROX. 2 LITRES WATER

korean red pepper and shredded pork

If fridge management had been a subject at school I would have been top of the class. Mine is an Aladdin's cave of condiments, preserved fruits and vegetables and pastes. The pastes are made from fresh herbs and spices. They give tongue-tingling bursts of flavour to favourite broths. Just dollop in a spoonful and stir. Made in advance, these pastes add special culinary signature to broths. If you were Korean you would use Gochujang in this recipe, a spicy, pungent fermented condiment made from red chilli, glutinous rice and fermented soybean. I use roasted peppers instead as Gochujang can be difficult to get hold of.

Preheat the oven to 220°C/200°C fan/gas mark 7.

First make the paste. Begin by roasting the pepper halves, skin side up, on a baking tray for 15 minutes. When the peppers are charred and blistered remove them from the oven and either finely chop or roughly blend them to a purée.

Heat the vegetable oil in a frying pan over a medium heat and gently fry the shallot, lemon grass, chilli, garlic, turmeric, lime leaves and fish sauce for a few minutes. Add the red pepper purée and simmer for 10 minutes, stirring occasionally so that it doesn't stick. Remove from the heat and allow to cool. You can make this paste in advance and store it in the fridge for up to 2 weeks in an airtight container.

Preheat the oven to 140°C/120°C fan/gas mark 2.

Smear the pork belly with the honey, fish sauce, tomato purée and ginger slices. Place on an oven tray on top of the star anise. Bake for 2 hours.

Remove the pork from the oven and allow to cool for a few minutes then shred with a couple of forks. (Or, if you want you can cook the pork belly in advance and store it, before shredding, in the fridge. You can reheat it in the oven at 140°C/120°C fan/gas mark 2 for 10 minutes or in the microwave.)

When you are ready to eat, cook the rice according to the packet instructions then cover and set aside to keep warm.

To bring it all together heat the stock in a large saucepan over a medium heat, add the pak choi and simmer for a minute. Add the shredded pork and coconut cream, stir in thoroughly.

Portion out the rice into bowls and add the broth. Stir in a heaped dessertspoon of red pepper paste into each portion, add a sprig of coriander and a glug of fish sauce if you like it salty!

serves 4

PER SERVING 835 KCALS, PROTEIN 39.2G, CARBS 41.8G, FAT 56G, SAT FAT 19.5G, FIBRE 3.5G, SUGAR 10.5G, SALT 1.3G

FOR THE PASTE

2 RED PEPPERS, SLICED IN HALF AND DESEEDED
50ML VEGETABLE OIL
1 SHALLOT, FINELY CHOPPED
½ LEMON GRASS STALK, FINELY SLICED
1 RED CHILLI, FINELY CHOPPED
3 CLOVES GARLIC, FINELY CHOPPED
2 PIECES (APPROX. 25G) OF FRESH TURMERIC ROOT, FINELY CHOPPED
2 LIME LEAVES, FINELY CHOPPED
15ML FISH SAUCE

FOR THE SHREDDED PORK

600G CUT OF PORK BELLY, SKIN AND BONES REMOVED
1 TEASPOON HONEY
15ML FISH SAUCE
15G TOMATO PURÉE
3CM PIECE (APPROX. 25G) OF FRESH GINGER ROOT, ROUGHLY SLICED
3 STAR ANISE

400G WHITE JASMINE RICE
600ML PORK RIB OR CHICKEN STOCK (SEE PAGES 36 AND 52)
2–3 HEADS OF PAK CHOI, WASHED AND ROUGHLY SLICED
100ML COCONUT CREAM

TO SERVE

SPRIGS OF FRESH CORIANDER
FISH SAUCE (OPTIONAL)

My kids eat bowls of this rich broth … strange, as they're not particularly keen on either tomatoes or onion. It's probably the pork and egg fritters fried in sesame oil that are so moreish! Pork fritters are great served with rice, too.

pork fritters in broth

Heat the stock in a large saucepan over a medium heat, add the tomatoes and shallots and simmer for 30 minutes until soft.

Mix the pork with the eggs, spring onions, hoisin sauce and a touch of soy sauce.

Heat 1 tablespoon of sesame oil and 1 tablespoon of vegetable oil in a large frying pan.

Lower a tablespoon of the pork mix into the oil and fry over medium heat until golden brown for 5 minutes on each side. Remove and drain on kitchen paper. Repeat until you've used up all the mix, adding more oil if you need to. You should end up with about 20 fritters.

Add the broccoli to the broth along with the fritters, simmer for a few minutes and voilà!

serves 4

PER SERVING 452 KCALS, PROTEIN 38.9G, CARBS 9.7G, FAT 27.5G, SAT FAT 6.3G, FIBRE 5.1G, SUGAR 8.6G, SALT 1.6G

750ML CHICKEN STOCK (SEE PAGE 52)
4 LARGE TOMATOES, SLICED
4 MEDIUM SHALLOTS, SLICED
20 SMALL BROCCOLI FLORETS

FOR THE FRITTERS
500G MINCED PORK
2 LARGE EGGS
3 SPRING ONIONS, SLICED
1 TABLESPOON HOISIN SAUCE
SOY SAUCE
SESAME OIL AND VEGETABLE OIL, FOR FRYING

It's important to walk the hills and follow ancient pathways. Last winter I found myself following trails untrodden for decades; encountering sinuous lakes stuffed with freshwater mussels the size of your fist. I paused with Henry, the farmer, and we surveyed an oxbow lake on his land. Henry explained how Victorian sluices work, shifting water from Winchester to Southampton, much of it hidden underground. I shared hot and sour meatball broth with him and he became quite animated. It was wonderful to take a few moments with a great conservationist, who buys land for the sole purpose of preserving it for future generations. Anyway, here's the recipe, perfect for the Thermos.

pork meatballs
in hot and sour broth

To make the meatballs mix the minced pork, spring onions, five spice, ginger, red chilli and fish sauce in a small bowl until sticky and slightly glutinous.

Wet your hands and form into balls the size of large cherry tomatoes. Makes about 24 balls.

Pour the stock into a large saucepan over a medium heat. Add the onion, pepper, garlic, vinegar, tomato purée and honey along with the meatballs and simmer for 15 minutes.

Add the rice and edamame beans. Simmer for a further minute or two and serve.

serves 2
PER SERVING 263 KCALS, PROTEIN 20.7G, CARBS 18.8G, FAT 10.8G, SAT FAT 2.5G, FIBRE 3.8G, SUGAR 10.4G, SALT 0.8G

FOR THE MEATBALLS
250G MINCED PORK
3 SPRING ONIONS, FINELY SLICED
1 TEASPOON FIVE-SPICE POWDER
2CM PIECE (APPROX. 15G) OF FRESH GINGER ROOT, FINELY CHOPPED
1 MEDIUM STRENGTH RED CHILLI, FINELY CHOPPED
20ML FISH SAUCE

FOR THE BROTH
400ML PORK RIB OR CHICKEN STOCK (SEE PAGES 36 AND 52)
1 LARGE ONION, ROUGHLY CHOPPED
1 RED PEPPER, ROUGHLY CHOPPED
3 CLOVES GARLIC, FINELY CHOPPED
2 TEASPOONS WHITE WINE VINEGAR
20G TOMATO PURÉE
15G HONEY
60G COOKED BROWN RICE
75G FROZEN EDAMAME BEANS (SOYA BEANS)

My son's favourite breakfast – prepared in minutes and eaten in seconds. We generally prepare the noodles in advance so they are ready in the fridge, keeping the chicken stock company.

sesame omelette and pork broth
with rice noodles

Briefly whisk the eggs with the sesame oil and a few drops of teriyaki sauce.

Heat the stock in a saucepan, add the carrot, broccoli and baby greens and simmer for 3 minutes.

Meanwhile, heat up the omelette pan, add a little sunflower oil to coat the base of the omelette pan and pour in the eggs. Give them a brief, frantic mix, and then cook for another minute until solid. Turn out onto a chopping board and slice into strips.

Throw the noodles into the stock – they will heat up immediately – and season with a little more teriyaki sauce. Finally, pour into a bowl and top with the sliced omelette.

I often garnish mine with a few slices of red chilli.

serves 1

PER SERVING 457 KCALS, PROTEIN 31.5G, CARBS 23.9G, FAT 25.1G, SAT FAT 3.7G, FIBRE 5.1G, SUGAR 4.8G, SALT 2.2G

YOU WILL NEED A SMALL, NON-STICK OMELETTE PAN

2 LARGE EGGS, CRACKED INTO A BOWL
1 TEASPOON SESAME OIL
TERIYAKI SAUCE
300ML PORK RIB OR CHICKEN STOCK (SEE PAGES 36 AND 52)
1 TABLESPOON GRATED CARROT
1 TABLESPOON PEELED AND GRATED BROCCOLI
A HANDFUL OF SNIPPED BABY GREENS, SUCH AS CAVOLO NERO OR KALE
SUNFLOWER OIL
A GENEROUS PORTION OF RICE NOODLES (SEE PAGE 13), COOKED AND READY TO GO, TOSSED IN A FEW DROPS OF SESAME OIL
RED CHILLI, SLICED (OPTIONAL)

Ultra-thin slices of belly pork give this porridge sweetness and texture. My wife said it tasted like Chinese spicy pork risotto, whatever that is.

savoury rice porridge
with pork

To prepare the pork belly place in the freezer for 1 hour until frozen but still cuttable. Then, with your sharpest knife, cut into ultra-thin slices – the thinner the slices the more tender they will be in the porridge. If you are not confident doing this, get your butcher or a friend with a steady hand to do it.

Boil the rice in the stock for 30 minutes until soft and porridgy.

Stir in the grated ginger, pork, hoisin and soy. Simmer for another 5–8 minutes until the pork is cooked.

Meanwhile dry-fry the sesame seeds in a small frying pan over a medium heat for a couple of minutes, stirring frequently until they are golden brown.

Serve sprinkled with the spring onions and sesame seeds.

serves 2–3

PER SERVING 523 KCALS, PROTEIN 30.2G, CARBS 33.3G, FAT 29.5G, SAT FAT 7.6G, FIBRE 1.7G, SUGAR 3.9G, SALT 1.7G

300G BONELESS PORK BELLY, SKIN REMOVED
100G WHITE SHORTGRAIN RICE
600ML PORK RIB OR CHICKEN STOCK (SEE PAGES 36 AND 52)
4CM PIECE (APPROX. 30G) OF FRESH GINGER ROOT, PEELED AND GRATED
1 LEVEL TABLESPOON HOISIN SAUCE
SOY SAUCE, TO TASTE
2 TEASPOONS SESAME SEEDS, PLUS EXTRA TO SERVE
4 SPRING ONIONS, WASHED AND SLICED

This naturally spiced broth is based on the Chinese recipe bah-kut-teh. The name literally translates as 'meat bone tea' – and this complex, hearty elixir always gives me a bit of a lift.

traditional pork rib broth
with cinnamon, cloves and star anise

Heat the oil in a frying pan over a medium heat and gently fry the shallots and garlic, stirring frequently, for about 10 minutes until crispy. Remove with a slotted spoon and drain on kitchen paper. Once cool, transfer to small bowl.

Heat the stock in a large saucepan and add the cavolo nero. Simmer for a minute or two. Add the brown rice and soy sauce to taste.

Ladle into bowls and top each portion with the crispy shallots.

serves 4

PER SERVING 591 KCALS, PROTEIN 33.4G, CARBS 44.8G, FAT 29.5G, SAT FAT 6G, FIBRE 6.4G, SUGAR 3.4G, SALT 2.2G

2 TABLESPOONS SUNFLOWER OR RAPESEED OIL
100G SHALLOTS, PEELED AND THINLY SLICED
4 CLOVES GARLIC, THINLY SLICED
400–500G COOKED SHORTGRAIN BROWN RICE
1.2 LITRES PORK RIB STOCK (SEE PAGE 36), STRAINED, INCLUDING THE RIBS
400G SHREDDED CAVOLO NERO
SOY SAUCE

My friend Marta taught me how to cook this incredible broth. It's a typically Polish recipe in the way it balances the sweetness of pork with sour cucumber and aromatic dill. Make sure you use firm, authentic Polish pickles in brine for this dish, otherwise it just won't work.

pork rib and pickled cucumber

Pour the stock into a large saucepan over a medium heat, add the ribs, celery, leek and parsley and simmer for about 1 hour 30 minutes.

Remove the ribs and allow to cool. Strain the stock using a conical strainer into another large saucepan and discard the vegetables and parsley.

Add the carrot and potatoes to the stock and simmer for 20 minutes. Then take the meat off the bone and add to the simmering broth.

Roughly grate the cucumbers, reserving the juices, then add to the broth with all the pickle juice that was released, along with the crème fraîche and dill. You may need a little salt and pepper. Serve with plenty of good rye bread.

serves 4

PER SERVING 764 KCALS, PROTEIN 58.6G, CARBS 16.9G, FAT 50.3G, SAT FAT 19.8G, FIBRE 4.5G, SUGAR 4.3G, SALT 2.9G

1 LITRE PORK RIB OR CHICKEN STOCK (SEE PAGES 36 AND 52)
1KG PORK RIBS
1 CELERY STICK
1 MEDIUM LEEK
A LARGE BUNCH OF FLAT-LEAF PARSLEY
2 MEDIUM CARROTS, PEELED AND DICED
2 LARGE POTATOES, PEELED AND DICED
6 MEDIUM PICKLED CUCUMBERS (APPROX. 300G)
100ML CRÈME FRAÎCHE
½ BUNCH OF FRESH DILL, CHOPPED
SALT AND FRESHLY GROUND BLACK PEPPER
RYE BREAD, TO SERVE

I once met a man who buries his cabbages in a deep pit, where they ferment for up to two years. He sells the final product finely sliced in little pots. It is the world's finest sauerkraut! Not all sauerkraut is made like this but the raw fermented type is a miraculous food, both good for you and utterly delicious! This is a traditional meal based on the Alsatian recipe, choucroûte.

sauerkraut broth
with ham hock and potatoes

Cook the potatoes in boiling water for 15 minutes until just tender but still firm. Drain.

Heat the stock in a medium saucepan. Give the sauerkraut a light squeeze to remove the liquid, then add it to the stock along with the ham hock and leeks. Simmer for 5 minutes until the leeks are soft.

Add the potatoes, sprinkle on the parsley and season with salt and pepper to taste.

serves 2

PER SERVING 436 KCALS, PROTEIN 40.7G, CARBS 28.8G, FAT 15.6G, SAT FAT 2G, FIBRE 8.8G, SUGAR 6.4G, SALT 4.5G

300G JERSEY ROYAL POTATOES OR OTHER NEW POTATOES
600ML PORK RIB OR CHICKEN STOCK (SEE PAGES 36 AND 52)
150G SAUERKRAUT (I USE A NATURALLY FERMENTED ONE FROM MY LOCAL HEALTH FOOD SHOP)
200G SHREDDED HAM HOCK (AVAILABLE PREPARED FROM MOST SUPERMARKETS)
200G LEEKS, WASHED AND SLICED
A SMALL BUNCH OF FLAT-LEAF PARSLEY, ROUGHLY CHOPPED
SALT AND FRESHLY GROUND BLACK PEPPER

Poultry

Chicken broth made from organic, free-range chicken reminds me of family and home. The aroma of simmering chicken bones draws us to the kitchen and it is an excellent pick-me-up when we are jaded or ill.

It is the most adaptable stock and can be used as a base for gravies, soups and sauces. I add pig's trotters for extra body, but these are optional.

Chicken wings, carcasses, necks and feet are all perfect for making chicken broth. Feet are highest in collagen, but are the most difficult part of the animal to obtain, so order in advance from the butcher or farmers' market.

I usually use raw unroasted bones, as the flavour adapts better to the recipes that call for chicken stock. The light meaty flavour allows the vegetables, herbs and spices to shine through. Roasted chicken bones are excellent for heartier broths, gravies and sauces. I call this my 'dirty' chicken stock and shovel all sorts of meat and vegetable leftovers into this stock. There's very little nutritional difference between a stock made with raw chicken bones and one made with roasted chicken bones.

This is my favourite stock as it is light, flavoursome and adapts to most dishes. If you're not that keen on pork omit the trotters; your stock won't set into a firm jelly but it will still taste perfectly delicious! If you prefer the flavour of roasted chicken bones you can reserve the carcasses from your roast dinner and keep them in the freezer until you make this stock.

chicken stock

As with most of my stock recipes, place all ingredients in a very large saucepan with enough water to cover everything and bring to the boil. Reduce the heat to a gentle simmer. You don't want the liquid to bubble away merrily as it will reduce too fast and the surface oil will mix with the stock, making it taste fatty.

Simmer for most of the day, minimum of 4 hours, preferably for 6–8 hours.

When the stock is ready the liquid will be clear and the meat melting off the bones. Pour the stock through a sieve into a large bowl and distribute into Tupperware pots with tight-fitting lids, using a ladle.

makes 4–4.5 litres
PER 100G
(WITH TROTTERS) 48 KCALS, PROTEIN 4.1G, CARBS 0.6G, FAT 3.2G, SAT FAT 0G, FIBRE 0.3G, SUGAR 0.4G, SALT 0.4G
(WITHOUT TROTTERS) 22 KCALS, PROTEIN 2.4G, CARBS 0.7G, FAT 1.1G, SAT FAT 0G, FIBRE 0.3G, SUGAR 0.5, SALT 0G

200G LEEKS, WASHED AND ROUGHLY SLICED
200G CELERY STICKS, SNAPPED INTO TWO OR THREE SHORT PIECES
300G CARROTS, WASHED BUT UNPEELED, ROUGHLY CHOPPED
300G ONIONS, UNPEELED BUT ROOT END REMOVED, ROUGHLY CHOPPED
1 HEAD OF GARLIC, SLICED IN HALF, ANY ROOTY BITS REMOVED
3KG RAW CHICKEN CARCASSES, INCLUDING WINGS AND NECKS, IF AVAILABLE
2 PIG'S TROTTERS (OPTIONAL)
APPROX. 5 LITRES WATER

Duck stock is deeper in flavour than chicken stock and is great for meaty stews.

duck stock

Follow the same method for the chicken stock.

makes 3 litres
PER 100G 11 KCALS, PROTEIN 0.7G, CARBS 0.9G, FAT 0.2G, SAT FAT 0G, FIBRE 0.3G, SUGAR 0.7, SALT 0G

2 CELERY STICKS, SNAPPED IN TWO
A SPRIG OF ROSEMARY
2 BAY LEAVES
A COUPLE OF SPRIGS OF THYME
A SMALL BUNCH OF FLAT-LEAF PARSLEY, INCLUDING STALKS (APPROX. 30G)
2 ONIONS, UNPEELED BUT ROOT END REMOVED, ROUGHLY CHOPPED
1 MEDIUM HEAD OF GARLIC, HALVED
4 MEDIUM CARROTS, WASHED BUT UNPEELED, ROUGHLY CHOPPED
2.5KG DUCK BONES
2 TEASPOONS (4G) PORCINI MUSHROOM POWDER OR DRIED PIECES
¼ BOTTLE RED WINE
50G TOMATO PURÉE
250G RIPE TOMATOES, HALVED
APPROX. 4 LITRES WATER

For this recipe both the polenta pancakes and roasted red pepper pesto can be made in advance, leaving you the simplest of tasks – to simmer thin slices of fennel and butternut squash in chicken broth until falling apart. Try topping the polenta pancakes with the pesto and dipping in the broth, a semi-religious experience!

chicken, red pepper and rosemary broth
with polenta pancakes

Weigh out the polenta into a medium bowl and add the eggs, rosemary, chilli, fennel seeds, salt, crème fraîche and baking powder. Whisk until smooth.

Heat a large frying pan over a low-medium heat and place as many pancake rings as you can in it, ensuring they remain flat against the frying surface (otherwise the polenta mix will run out).

Pour a few drops of olive oil into each ring followed by 5mm of polenta mix. Slowly fry until bubbles have formed on top of the pancakes and they look set, approximately 5 minutes.

Remove the rings (using a tea towel to protect your fingers) and turn the pancakes over. Cook for a further minute or two until golden brown on each side. Repeat with the remaining batter until you have 12 pancakes.

To make the red pepper and rosemary pesto, put all the ingredients in a blender and whizz until smooth, approximately 30 seconds.

To make the broth, simmer the chicken, butternut squash and fennel in the chicken stock for 20 minutes or until all the ingredients are cooked. Season with salt and pepper.

Ladle into wide bowls and serve each portion with a tablespoon of red pepper pesto and a small pile of polenta pancakes.

serves 4
PER SERVING 566 KCALS, PROTEIN 52.3G, CARBS 29G, FAT 25.2G, SAT FAT 7.7G, FIBRE 7.4G, SUGAR 4.9G, SALT 2.8G

FOR THE POLENTA PANCAKES
100G POLENTA
2 LARGE EGGS
A SMALL SPRIG OF FRESH ROSEMARY, CHOPPED
A PINCH OF FLAKED RED CHILLI, IDEALLY SMOKED
½ TEASPOON FENNEL SEEDS, LIGHTLY CRUSHED
   USING A PESTLE AND MORTAR
½ TEASPOON SALT
80G CRÈME FRAÎCHE
½ TEASPOON BAKING POWDER
OLIVE OIL

FOR THE RED PEPPER AND ROSEMARY PESTO
150G ROASTED RED PEPPERS
30G SALTED ANCHOVY FILLETS (ABOUT 6)
1 TEASPOON CAPERS
A SMALL SPRIG OF ROSEMARY
1 SMALL CLOVE GARLIC
10ML AGED BALSAMIC VINEGAR
JUICE OF ½ LEMON

3 SKINLESS BONELESS CHICKEN BREASTS, SLICED
½ MEDIUM BUTTERNUT SQUASH, PEELED AND THINLY
   SLICED
2 LARGE FENNEL BULBS, THINLY SLICED
800ML CHICKEN STOCK (SEE PAGE 52)
SALT AND FRESHLY GROUND BLACK PEPPER

This broth tastes clean and ever so fresh, and is perfect as a light lunch or early evening meal. You can cook the quinoa and shred the chicken in advance. When you return home, simply heat the stock, throw in the ingredients and voilà! A steaming bowl of lean, delicious food is ready. If you like a little spice in your life serve with sriracha, a hot chilli and garlic sauce.

savoury quinoa chicken broth
with kale

Heat the stock in a large saucepan over a medium heat, add the chicken breasts and simmer for 15 minutes, then remove them from the stock and allow to cool for 10 minutes.

Hand shred the meat and either return to the stock or place in the fridge in an airtight container until needed, no longer than 2 days. Likewise, you can cool and store the stock in the fridge after this stage.

To finish off your dish heat the stock in a large saucepan, add the chicken and kale and simmer for 2–3 minutes. Add the petits pois and quinoa and heat for a further couple of minutes until steaming hot but not boiling.

Serve in deep bowls with sriracha sauce, if you wish.

serves 4

PER SERVING 504 KCALS, PROTEIN 63.5G, CARBS 24G, FAT 14.7G, SAT FAT 1.5G, FIBRE 11.2G, SUGAR 3.9G, SALT 1.5G

1 LITRE CHICKEN STOCK (SEE PAGE 52)
4 MEDIUM SKINLESS, BONELESS CHICKEN BREASTS
400G KALE, THOROUGHLY WASHED AND THICK
   STALKS REMOVED, THEN SHREDDED
250G PETITS POIS
400G COOKED QUINOA (I OFTEN USE A MIX OF RED,
   WHITE AND BLACK, BUT THEN I DO GET CARRIED
   AWAY...)
A SWIRL OF SRIRACHA SAUCE (OPTIONAL), TO SERVE

Tamarind is a bean-shaped fruit filled with dark, sticky sweet pulp. It imparts a deep fruitiness into this luxurious broth. Preparing tamarind is usually a messy business – but not in this recipe! You simply simmer the sticky pods in stock and strain off the goodness. Served with a simple lime salsa, this broth is a meal in itself.

duck and tamarind broth
with rice and salsa

Mix the ingredients for the salsa together in a small bowl and set aside.

Coat the duck breasts with the sesame seeds and teriyaki sauce. Place, skin-side down, in a dry frying pan and gently fry for about 10 minutes. Turn over and cook for a further 3 minutes. Leave in the pan until needed.

Meanwhile heat the duck stock with the tamarind. Whisk as it simmers until the tamarind pulp has dissolved leaving the seeds and pith. Strain off the stock, discard the unsightly bits and return to the saucepan.

Add the broccoli and simmer for 3 minutes until cooked but al dente. Add the rice and simmer to heat, then pour into a serving dish.

Slice the duck on top and serve with the salsa and extra teriyaki sauce, if you wish.

serves 4
PER SERVING 689 KCALS, PROTEIN 61.8G, CARBS 48.3G, FAT 25.9G, SAT FAT 7.6G, FIBRE 5.7G, SUGAR 13.9G, SALT 1G

FOR THE SALSA
½ RED ONION, DICED
JUICE OF 1 LIME
½ RED PEPPER, CORED, DESEEDED AND DICED
½ YELLOW PEPPER, CORED, DESEEDED AND DICED
A SMALL BUNCH OF CORIANDER, STALKS REMOVED, WASHED AND CHOPPED

FOR THE BROTH
3–4 UNSKINNED DUCK BREASTS, SKIN LIGHTLY SCORED WITH A KNIFE
1 TABLESPOON SESAME SEEDS
1 TABLESPOON TERIYAKI SAUCE, PLUS EXTRA FOR SERVING IF DESIRED
1 LITRE DUCK STOCK (SEE PAGE 52)
12 TAMARIND, CRUNCHY OUTER SHELL REMOVED
400G LONG-STEM BROCCOLI
400–500G COOKED LONG GRAIN WHITE RICE

A white bean broth, flavoured with yellow chillies, fresh turmeric and tomato, soured with lime juice and topped with crispy polenta-coated chicken breast.

peruvian lime and chilli broth

with chicken

Preheat the oven to 180°C/160°C fan/gas mark 4.

Place the tomatoes on a baking dish, season with salt and olive oil and roast in the oven for 30 minutes.

Heat the stock. Add the tomatoes, turmeric, ají amarillo, lime juice, beans and a touch of salt, if needed. Simmer for 3–5 minutes.

Meanwhile, mix together the turmeric powder, polenta and 1 teaspoon of salt. Use the mixture to coat the chicken breasts. Heat a non-stick frying pan and add the vegetable oil. Fry the chicken breasts over a medium heat for 8 minutes on each side until golden brown and cooked through.

Pour the broth into a serving dish and slice the chicken breasts on top. Garnish with the coriander leaves.

serves 4

PER SERVING 469 KCALS, PROTEIN 62G, CARBS 20.2G, FAT 13.6G, SAT FAT 1.6G, FIBRE 8.6G, SUGAR 4.7G, SALT 2.8G

200G YELLOW CHERRY TOMATOES, CUT IN HALF
200G RED CHERRY TOMATOES, CUT IN HALF
SALT
OLIVE OIL
1 LITRE CHICKEN STOCK (SEE PAGE 52)
A SMALL PIECE (APPROX. 15G) OF FRESH TURMERIC ROOT, PEELED AND FINELY CHOPPED (WEAR GLOVES WHILE DOING THIS TO AVOID THE REALISTIC NICOTINE STAINS)
¼ TEASPOON AJI AMARILLO POWDER (PERUVIAN YELLOW CHILLI), IF AVAILABLE, OR USE 1 TEASPOON FINELY CHOPPED FRESH HOT RED CHILLI
JUICE OF 1 LIME
400G TIN SMALL WHITE BEANS, DRAINED (CANNELLINI ARE PERFECT)
2 TEASPOONS TURMERIC POWDER
1 TABLESPOON POLENTA
4 UNSKINNED CHICKEN BREASTS
2 TABLESPOONS VEGETABLE OIL
A SMALL BUNCH OF FRESH CORIANDER, LEAVES PLUCKED FROM STALKS, TO GARNISH

I love this warming broth, simmered with medicinal roots and seeds. Most of you who have been unwell will respond to this gentle recipe. Restorative food should taste good and not sit heavily on the stomach, so there's no chilli or other fiery ingredients here.

chinese health broth
with thinly sliced chicken breast

Put the chicken stock into a large saucepan. Crush the fennel seeds and aniseed using a pestle and mortar, then add all the ingredients to the stock and bring to a simmer over a medium heat.

After 20 minutes remove the chicken breasts and allow to cool enough to slice thinly.

Simmer the rest of the ingredients for a further hour, topping up the chicken stock with water or extra stock if necessary.

Return the chicken to the pan, remove the ginseng and serve immediately.

serves 2

PER SERVING 521 KCALS, PROTEIN 64.9G, CARBS 26.4G, FAT 16.5G, SAT FAT 1.9G, FIBRE 3.9G, SUGAR 5G, SALT 2G

1 LITRE CHICKEN STOCK (SEE PAGE 52)
½ TEASPOON FENNEL SEEDS
½ TEASPOON ANISEED
2 SKINLESS, BONELESS CHICKEN BREASTS
8 SHIITAKE MUSHROOMS, SLICED
2CM PIECE (APPROX. 15G) OF FRESH GINGER ROOT, GRATED
1 TABLESPOON RICE VINEGAR
20G DRIED GINSENG ROOT
1 TABLESPOON GOJI BERRIES
4 CLOVES GARLIC, PEELED

Is Bone Broth Paleo Food or Modern Food?

Most of the vegetables we buy today weren't available in prehistoric times. Tomatoes didn't arrive until the nineteenth century and avocados and red peppers weren't generally available until the 1960s. Maize was grown in the UK from about 3,500 BC, but we wouldn't recognise it as edible nowadays – not in this world of straight bananas and perfect apples. Cucumbers were spiny, lettuce was bitter; peas were so unbearably starchy and unpalatable that they needed boiling and peeling. Sea kale was the only cabbage available and beans were laced with cyanide.

Life for Paleolithic hunters was difficult and they would have supplemented the early cultivated grains and hunted meat with foraged berries, herbs and mushrooms. I argue that these nomads would only infrequently return from the hunt laden with meat and that famine and malnutrition would have been rife.

We have a fanciful image of bones boiling over an open fire but the more likely way of treating meat was to air dry, sun dry, salt or smoke to preserve it for the scarce winter months. If Paleolithic man had made bone broth it would have been lacking the flavours of cultivated vegetables that make our bone broths so delicious today.

A light, delicate broth featuring tomato concasse – which is chopped, skinless tomato with the seeds removed. The outer flesh of a tomato is sweeter than the tangy interior, perfect for this restorative broth.

chicken, tomato and lemongrass broth

Put the chicken stock in a saucepan over a moderate heat. Add the lemongrass slices and the chicken breasts and simmer for 20 minutes until the meat is cooked. Remove the breasts and allow to cool before slicing. This can be done in advance and the chicken kept in an airtight container in the fridge for up to 2 days. Strain and reserve the chicken stock but discard the lemongrass.

Drop the tomatoes into a pan of boiling water for 10 seconds. Remove with a slotted spoon and transfer quickly to a bowl of iced water. The skin will immediately start to peel. Remove all the skin from the tomatoes with your fingers or a paring knife and cut the flesh into quarters. Squeeze out all the seeds and chop the tomato into small pieces. You can chuck any scraps of leftover tomato into your next stockpot.

Reheat the chicken stock if necessary. Simmer the tomato and the sliced chicken breast in the stock for 5 minutes, add the fish sauce and it's ready.

Delicious served with jasmine rice.

serves 2
PER SERVING 353 KCALS, PROTEIN 53.4G, CARBS 14.1G, FAT 8G, SAT FAT 1.6G, FIBRE 5.7G, SUGAR 12.4G, SALT 0.9G

500ML CHICKEN STOCK (SEE PAGE 52)
2 LEMONGRASS STALKS, ROUGHLY SLICED
2 SKINLESS, BONELESS CHICKEN BREASTS
5 LARGE RIPE TOMATOES, SCORED WITH A KNIFE
2 TEASPOONS FISH SAUCE
JASMINE RICE (OPTIONAL), TO SERVE

I've hijacked the traditional minestrone recipe and created this delightfully satisfying broth. You can stand a spoon up in minestrone. This recipe certainly passes that test!

chicken minestrone

Put all the ingredients, apart from the beans and salt and pepper in a large saucepan. Simmer for 30 minutes until soft and meltingly good.

Add the beans and season. At this point you can stir it up so that the bean mush incorporates into the broth, giving it more body.

Serve topped with shaved Parmesan if you wish.

serves 4

PER SERVING 308 KCALS, PROTEIN 34G, CARBS 22.3G, FAT 6.3G, SAT FAT 1G, FIBRE 10.7G, SUGAR 8.5G, SALT 1.7G

1 LITRE CHICKEN STOCK (SEE PAGE 52)
4 SKINLESS, BONELESS CHICKEN THIGHS, CUT INTO APPROX. 1CM DICE
2 CELERY STICKS, THINLY SLICED
2 MEDIUM CARROTS, PEELED AND DICED
1 MEDIUM POINTY RED PEPPER, DICED
300G CHERRY TOMATOES, CUT IN HALF
40G TOMATO PURÉE
5 SAGE LEAVES, FINELY CHOPPED
1 TEASPOON FINELY CHOPPED ROSEMARY
2 SPRIGS OF THYME, FINELY CHOPPED
400G TIN OF CANNELLINI BEANS
SALT AND FRESHLY GROUND BLACK PEPPER
SHAVED PARMESAN (OPTIONAL), TO SERVE

The History of Food in a Thousand Broths

Broths have encapsulated the best and worst of food over the ages. Swindlers have adulterated them, famous chefs have adulated them. Fine consommés have been served to aristocracy, whereas the poor have been prescribed thin broths with few, if any, nutrients. Life was grim, as emphasised by Sir Hugh Platt in 1596 when extemporising on remedies against famine. 'Boile your beans and pease ... in faire water ... and the second or third boyling, you shall find a strange alteration in taste, for the water hath sucked out the greater part of their rankness....'

During Tudor times the wealthy feasted on meats, rich broths and exotic, imported food items while the poor suffered from vitamin deficiencies, ergotism and starvation. The fortunes and misfortunes of man were contained within a bowl. Broths can make a little food go a long way or concentrate the flavour of meat and bones into a drop of golden goodness.

Stracciatella is a term to describe a traditional Italian broth, thickened with stringy shreds of egg and Parmesan (stracciatella means little shreds). I admit this isn't the healthiest broth in the world, but it's quick, easy and incredibly satisfying in a short-term indulgent sort of way. I've added baby spinach leaves to make you feel slightly less guilty!

stracciatella with chicken
and fettuccini

Put the chicken breasts in the stock and simmer for 20 minutes until cooked through. Remove from the stock, allow to cool slightly, then shred using two forks. (This can be done in advance. Cooked, the chicken breasts will keep in an airtight container in the fridge for up to 3 days).

Heat the chicken broth in a medium saucepan with the shredded chicken and spinach.

Whisk together the eggs, crème fraîche, nutmeg, white pepper, Parmesan and lemon zest in a small bowl.

As the broth simmers away, slowly pour in the egg mix in a steady stream, whisking as you go. Once all the egg has been added, immediately remove from the heat.

Pour into bowls of steaming fettuccine. Add extra Parmesan if you wish, as the Italians do!

serves 2

PER SERVING 655 KCALS, PROTEIN 61.1G, CARBS 33.5G, FAT 29.5G, SAT FAT 13.6G, FIBRE 4.7G, SUGAR 3.2G, SALT 1.2G

2 SMALL SKINLESS, BONELESS CHICKEN BREASTS
500ML CHICKEN STOCK (SEE PAGE 52)
100G BABY SPINACH OR CHARD, FINELY SHREDDED
2 EGGS
50G FULL FAT CRÈME FRAÎCHE
ABOUT ¼ NUTMEG, GRATED
A PINCH OF WHITE PEPPER
40G FINELY GRATED PARMESAN, PLUS EXTRA TO SERVE
ZEST OF ½ LEMON
200G FRESHLY COOKED FETTUCCINE

It may seem odd to suggest that you cook up the very stew that's responsible for the colossal size of Japan's Sumo wrestlers. *Chanko-nabe* is a Japanese protein- and carb-laden stew eaten in enormous quantities along with beer, rice and sake, followed by a refreshing nap. In Japan *chanko-nabe* is traditionally prepared by junior Sumo wrestlers who end up eating last, after the high-ranking Sekitori. This version is lighter and should be served with a small portion of rice (and less beer, perhaps).

I like the idea of communal one-pot eating and flexible recipes. Here's my version of *Chanko-nabe*.

japanese chicken stew
chanko-nabe

Put the chicken stock into a large saucepan with the chicken, carrots, mooli, shiitake mushrooms, potato and leeks. Bring to a simmer and cook for 30 minutes until cooked.

Add the miso, pak choi, tofu, mirin and teriyaki sauce. Simmer for 1 minute and it's ready.

Serve with fluffy white rice!

serves 2
PER SERVING 400 KCALS, PROTEIN 46.2G, CARBS 28.8G, FAT 9.7G, SAT FAT 1.7G, FIBRE 6.5G, SUGAR 13.1G, SALT 1.5G

800ML CHICKEN STOCK (SEE PAGE 52)
6 BONELESS CHICKEN THIGHS, CUT INTO CHUNKS
4 CARROTS, PEELED AND DICED
1 SMALL MOOLI, SHREDDED
10 SHIITAKE MUSHROOMS, SLICED
1 LARGE, UNPEELED POTATO, WASHED AND DICED
2 LEEKS, WASHED AND SLICED
2 TABLESPOONS WHITE MISO PASTE (OR ANY MISO IF YOU CAN'T GET HOLD OF WHITE)
200G PAK CHOI OR OTHER ORIENTAL GREENS
200G SMOKED TOFU, SLICED 5MM THICK
2 TABLESPOONS MIRIN
1 TABLESPOON TERIYAKI SAUCE
STEAMED WHITE RICE, TO SERVE (SEE PAGE 13)

This is an old Irish broth, thickened with egg yolks, featuring shredded chicken, peas, lettuce and spice mix, unearthed in *Cassell's Dictionary of Cookery* (1877). This is now one of my favourite broths and I became quite emotional when the recipe actually worked! Both the chicken and the potatoes can be cooked in advance for this recipe. It is a hearty dish, beautifully quick to make, and with the flavour of sweet spice. Who would have thought that 'sweet herbs' refers to that intriguing mélange of nutmeg, all spice, cinnamon and lavender?

balnamoon skink

Boil the potatoes for 15 minutes until cooked, then drain.

Meanwhile, if you are using uncooked chicken, simmer the thighs in the stock for 15 minutes, until cooked, then remove and leave to cool before shredding the meat by hand.

Put the stock, potatoes, shredded chicken, nutmeg, cinnamon, allspice, lavender, salt and pepper in a large saucepan over a medium heat and simmer for 10 minutes to let the flavours infuse.

Add the petits pois, bring to the boil and then remove from the heat and let it cool for a minute before adding the lettuce.

Slowly pour in the egg yolks, whisking the broth constantly as you do so. Serve immediately in large bowls.

serves 2

PER SERVING 461 KCALS, PROTEIN 56.5G, CARBS 21.3G, FAT 15.1G, SAT FAT 3.6G, FIBRE 7G, SUGAR 5G, SALT 3.1G

200G NEW POTATOES, ROUGHLY DICED
2 LARGE SKINLESS CHICKEN THIGHS (OR USE LEFTOVER ROAST CHICKEN THIGH MEAT)
500ML CHICKEN STOCK (SEE PAGE 52)
¼ NUTMEG, GRATED
1 CINNAMON STICK
¼ TEASPOON GROUND ALLSPICE
1 TEASPOON CHOPPED LAVENDER FLOWER OR LEAF
1 TEASPOON SALT AND ¼ TEASPOON GROUND WHITE PEPPER
150G PETITS POIS
6 LARGE CRUNCHY LETTUCE LEAVES, SHREDDED (OR USE BABY SPRING GREENS)
2 EGG YOLKS, LIGHTLY WHISKED

An authentic matzo ball relies on a good dose of
'*schmaltz*' – that's chicken fat to you and me.

matzo ball broth

Heat the stock in a large saucepan over a moderate heat and add the chicken breasts. Simmer for 15 minutes until cooked, then remove and leave to cool before shredding the meat by hand.

Meanwhile make the matzo balls. Mix all the ingredients together in a large bowl using a sturdy spoon. Gather into balls the size of walnuts and squeeze firmly so that all the ingredients are holding together. This recipe should make at least 20 balls.

Drop the matzo balls into the hot stock along with the carrot and celery and gently simmer for 20 minutes.

Add the shredded chicken and parsley, bring briefly to the boil and serve immediately.

serves 4

PER SERVING 510 KCALS, PROTEIN 42.6G, CARBS 42.5G, FAT 18G, SAT FAT 4.7G, FIBRE 3.5G, SUGAR 4.5G, SALT 1.8G

750ML CHICKEN STOCK (SEE PAGE 52)
2 SKINLESS CHICKEN BREASTS
1 LARGE CARROT, PEELED AND SLICED
2 CELERY STICKS, SLICED
12G ROUGHLY CHOPPED FLAT-LEAF PARSLEY

FOR THE MATZO BALLS
150G COARSE MATZO MEAL
2 LARGE EGGS
1 HEAPED TABLESPOON SCHMALTZ (CHICKEN FAT)
1 TEASPOON SALT FLAKES (I USE MALDON) AND A
    COUPLE OF TWISTS OF BLACK PEPPER
¼ TEASPOON BICARBONATE OF SODA
A SCRUNCHED-UP HANDFUL OF FLAT-LEAF PARSLEY,
    ROUGHLY CHOPPED
1 HEAPED TABLESPOON PLAIN FLOUR, PLUS
    1 TEASPOON
1 TABLESPOON COLD WATER

This recipe is a tantalising combination of duck stock, sweetened with pomegranate molasses, crispy duck leg and spicy pesto.

quick confit duck
with aubergine

Preheat the oven to 150°C/130°C fan/gas mark 2.

Rub the duck legs with 1 teaspoon of salt and some pepper, the thyme and oil.

To make the pesto, dry-fry the sesame seeds and fennel seeds over a gentle heat for 3–4 minutes, stirring constantly until golden brown. Use a pestle and mortar to pound the seeds with the thyme, salt and paprika until the thyme has been incorporated into the seed mix. Transfer to a small bowl and stir in the olive oil. This pesto can be stored in a cool larder or the fridge for up to 1 month in a sealed jar.

Bake the duck in the oven for 1½ hours, until golden brown and tender.

Towards the end of the duck cooking time simmer the aubergine slices in the stock for 20 minutes until tender. Add the molasses and season with salt. Stir in the quinoa.

Once the duck is out of the oven, shred the meat off the bone with a fork. Serve the broth in bowls topped with the shredded duck and a teaspoon of pesto.

serves 2

PER SERVING 497 KCALS, PROTEIN 23.9G, CARBS 35.5G, FAT 27G, SAT FAT 4.2G, FIBRE 8.4G, SUGAR 13.2G, SALT 4G

2 DUCK LEGS
SALT AND FRESHLY GROUND BLACK PEPPER
2 TEASPOONS CHOPPED FRESH THYME
A SMIDGEN OF OLIVE OIL
300G AUBERGINE, SLICED 5MM THICK
500ML DUCK STOCK OR CHICKEN STOCK
  (SEE PAGE 52)
2 TEASPOONS POMEGRANATE MOLASSES
200G COOKED MIXED QUINOA
  (OR RICE, IF YOU PREFER)

FOR THE PESTO
1 TABLESPOON SESAME SEEDS
1 TEASPOON FENNEL SEEDS
1 TABLESPOON ROUGHLY CHOPPED FRESH THYME
½ TEASPOON SALT
½ TEASPOON HOT SMOKED PAPRIKA
2 TABLESPOONS OLIVE OIL

This broth is a simple combination of tender chicken breast, baby leeks and freekeh. Back in the sixteenth century, cock-a-leekie was Scotland's national dish, using available produce to make a one-pot, sustaining feast. The original recipe used pearl barley, which I've replaced with greenwheat freekeh, a nutritious grain related to wheat, harvested young and lightly toasted. Take care when preparing the tender young baby leeks as the stalks can hide grit, so do wash them thoroughly.

cock-a-leekie

Gently fry the onion in the olive oil, stirring occasionally, until soft and sweet, about 15 minutes.

Meanwhile put the stock in a large saucepan over a moderate heat, add the chicken breasts along with the thyme and bay leaf and simmer for 15 minutes, until the meat is cooked through. Remove the chicken breast, allow to cool then slice.

Add the baby leeks and freekeh to the chicken stock and simmer for 5 minutes. Season the broth with salt and pepper, if needed.

Return the chicken breast to the pan and allow to heat through. Serve in big bowls with a dollop of red onion and topped with flat-leaf parsley. Good with either with crusty bread or oat pancakes.

serves 4

PER SERVING 528 KCALS, PROTEIN 61.8G, CARBS 33.2G, FAT 14.3G, SAT FAT 2.2G, FIBRE 9.7G, SUGAR 8.5G, SALT 3G

1 MEDIUM RED ONION, PEELED AND SLICED
1 TABLESPOON OLIVE OIL
600ML CHICKEN STOCK (SEE PAGE 52)
2 SKINLESS, BONELESS CHICKEN BREASTS
A SMALL BUNCH OF THYME
1 BAY LEAF
6–8 BABY LEEKS, CUT LENGTHWAYS, WASHED AND
     CAREFULLY INSPECTED FOR GRIT
200G COOKED FREEKEH (APPROX. 80G DRY WEIGHT,
     SIMMERED FOR 30 MINUTES)
SALT AND FRESHLY GROUND BLACK PEPPER
A SCRUNCHED UP HANDFUL OF FLAT-LEAF PARSLEY,
     ROUGHLY CHOPPED

I love the fragrant overtones of liquorice and aniseed in garden tarragon. I only ever use a few snips of it all season, so here's a naughty recipe with home-prepared artichoke hearts, soft-boiled eggs and rich crème fraîche. Boiled for 6 minutes your eggs will serenely occupy the border between hard and soft, to borrow a Japanese expression from a waitress at Yashin Sushi in South Kensington.

decadent tarragon chicken

Put the new potatoes in a small to medium thick-bottomed saucepan with ½ teaspoon of salt and 1 tablespoon of olive oil and cover with the lid. Cook over a low heat for 30 minutes, giving the pan an occasional shake, until the potatoes are soft.

Put the chicken in a bowl with the tarragon, lemon juice, tomato purée, garlic, salt and pepper and stir to coat. Just cover the base of a small frying pan with olive oil and fry the chicken over a medium heat for 10 minutes on each side until cooked through. Remove from the heat and, when cool enough to handle, cut into slices.

Meanwhile, prepare the artichokes. Cut the stalk to within a centimetre of the heart. Slice through the heart horizontally, half-way up the flower. Turn upside down on a chopping board so that the stalk is facing up and run a sharp knife down the outside, cutting away the indigestible outer leaf and revealing the tender heart. Do this all the way around each artichoke and then cut into quarters.

Drop the prepared artichokes into a pan of simmering water and cook for 10 minutes until soft. Drain and toss in the vinegar and a pinch of salt.

Heat the chicken stock in a saucepan. Add the crème fraîche and season with a little salt and pepper.

Take 2 bowls and load with sliced egg, potato, artichoke heart, sliced chicken breast and top up with chicken stock. Serve garnished with the reserved tarragon leaves.

serves 2

PER SERVING 791 KCALS, PROTEIN 43.1G, CARBS 22.8G, FAT 58.1G, SAT FAT 22.1G, FIBRE 2.3G, SUGAR 4.6G, SALT 3.7G

300G BABY NEW POTATOES

SALT

OLIVE OIL

2 SKINLESS CHICKEN BREASTS OR BONELESS CHICKEN THIGHS

A SMALL BUNCH OF TARRAGON LEAVES, A FEW RESERVED AS GARNISH, THE REST CHOPPED

JUICE OF ½ LEMON

1 TEASPOON TOMATO PURÉE

1 CLOVE GARLIC, FINELY CHOPPED

FRESHLY GROUND BLACK PEPPER

4 BABY ARTICHOKES

A SPLASH OF WHITE WINE VINEGAR (ABOUT 2 TEASPOONS)

500ML CHICKEN STOCK (SEE PAGE 52)

100ML FULL FAT CRÈME FRAÎCHE

2 LARGE EGGS, BOILED FOR 6 MINUTES, PLUNGED UNDER COLD RUNNING WATER AND PEELED

This broth is made with a not-too-hot spice paste with loads of character. If you have some leftover in the fridge, try serving with sautéed potatoes or as a marinade for lamb. Using various coloured cherry tomatoes makes the broth look pretty.

chicken with Saharan spice

First make the paste. Dry-toast the cardamom pods, coriander and cumin seeds in a pan over a medium heat for 3–4 minutes until they are slightly coloured and the aromas fill the kitchen. Crush the seeds using a pestle and mortar. Remove the outer husk of the cardamom pods, leaving the seeds.

Tip the seeds into a small bowl and add the garlic, turmeric, nutmeg, za'atar, lemon juice, tomato purée, salt, olive oil and chilli. Mix to a paste. This gorgeous sensuous Saharan spice mix can be stored in the fridge in an airtight container for 3–4 weeks.

Put the chicken strips into a bowl with 2 heaped teaspoons of the spice paste and stir to coat on all sides. Heat a little olive oil in a frying pan over a moderate heat, add the chicken strips and fry, turning occasionally for about 10 minutes, until cooked all the way through.

Heat the chicken stock in a large saucepan along with the chickpeas, courgettes and cherry tomatoes. Simmer for 5 minutes.

Portion into bowls and stir in a heaped teaspoon of paste into each portion and top with the chicken breast strips and mint leaves.

serves 4

PER SERVING 538 KCALS, PROTEIN 61G, CARBS 24.6G, FAT 19.8G, SAT FAT 3.3G, FIBRE 8.9G, SUGAR 7.4G, SALT 2.1G

2 SKINLESS, BONELESS CHICKEN BREASTS, CUT INTO STRIPS
OLIVE OIL
400ML CHICKEN STOCK (SEE PAGE 52)
200G COOKED CHICKPEAS
2 MEDIUM COURGETTES, DICED
200G CHERRY TOMATOES, SLICED
MINT LEAVES

FOR THE PASTE
3 CARDAMOM PODS
1 TEASPOON WHOLE CORIANDER SEEDS
1 TEASPOON CUMIN SEEDS
2 CLOVES GARLIC, FINELY CHOPPED
1 HEAPED TEASPOON TURMERIC POWDER
¼ NUTMEG, GRATED
½ TEASPOON GROUND ZA'ATAR
JUICE OF ½ LEMON
30G TOMATO PURÉE
½ TEASPOON SALT
40ML OLIVE OIL
½ TEASPOON DRIED FLAKED RED CHILLIES, NOT TOO HOT (OR SMOKED PAPRIKA IF YOU LIKE)

Fish

I have to say that a delicately scented fish stock is one of the most gratifying tonics on the planet. Oily fish don't make good stock but most other fish bones are perfect for the stockpot along with shellfish and crustaceans.

Fish bones for stock should be fresh or freshly frozen. I fillet fresh fish and store the bones in the freezer. Once I have around a kilo of bones I'm ready to make stock.

Herring, mackerel, sardines and salmon are the highest producers of Omega 3 fatty acids, which help lower cholesterol for a healthy heart and have a beneficial effect on brain structure. They are not produced naturally, so you need to get them from another source. Most fish offer decent amounts, as well as collagen and essential minerals. And, to the chef, fish bones are the building blocks for great broth!

We're especially good at catching fish these days. Beam trawling and other 'efficient' fishing methods have done a fairly good job at emptying oceans, so if you want to be ethical about the fish you eat, you can consult the Marine Stewardship Council or the Marine Conservation Society for the fish to eat and the fish to avoid.

This is a really useful stock to have in the fridge as it can be used to make seafood and fish broths that are a feature of Mediterranean cooking from Spain to Turkey. This stock is also used as a base for *brodetto*, a delicious fish stew from Italy (see page 91).

mediterranean fish stock

Place all the ingredients in a large saucepan with enough water to cover everything and put the lid firmly on. Gently boil for 35–40 minutes until the fish is falling apart and the vegetables are soft.

Strain through a conical sieve into a large bowl. Make sure you squeeze every drop of goodness out of the stock by pressing down using the back of a spoon. Ladle into airtight containers.

Once chilled this stock will keep for a week in the fridge.

makes 1 litre

PER 100G 17 KCALS, PROTEIN 0.8G, CARBS 1.4G, FAT 0.3G, SAT FAT 0G, FIBRE 0.7G, SUGAR 1.3G, SALT 0G

1KG SEA BASS BONES OR FLATFISH BONES, SAY PLAICE OR LEMON SOLE (NOT FROM OILY FISH, SUCH AS MACKEREL OR HERRING)
150G SHALLOTS, FINELY SLICED
100G LEEKS, FINELY SLICED
100G CELERY STICKS, FINELY SLICED
100G FENNEL BULB, FINELY SLICED
200G CARROTS, CLEANED AND FINELY SLICED
1 TEASPOON FENNEL SEEDS
½ TEASPOON SMOKED CHILLI POWDER
150G FRESH, SWEET CHERRY TOMATOES
60G TOMATO PURÉE
200ML DRY WHITE WINE
2 BAY LEAVES
A SMALL HANDFUL OF FRESH THYME
A SMALL BUNCH OF FLAT-LEAF PARSLEY
APPROX. 750ML WATER

This stock is a typical 'court bouillon', a French term meaning 'short broth' and is a kitchen classic. It is cooked for a fraction of the time of a slow-cooked broth to preserve the delicate flavours and is perfect as a base for a wide variety of fish and noodle dishes.

white fish stock

Place all the ingredients in a medium saucepan with enough water to cover everything and put the lid firmly on. Gently boil for 35–40 minutes until the fish is falling apart and the vegetables are soft.

Strain through a conical sieve into a large bowl and ladle into airtight containers.

Once chilled this stock will keep for a week in the fridge.

makes 1 litre
PER 100G 16 KCALS, PROTEIN 0.7G, CARBS 1.1G, FAT 0.3G, SAT FAT 0G, FIBRE 0.6G, SUGAR 0.9G, SALT 0G

1KG SEA BASS BONES OR FLATFISH BONES, SAY PLAICE
   OR LEMON SOLE
150G SHALLOTS, FINELY SLICED
100G LEEKS, FINELY SLICED
100G CELERY STICKS, FINELY SLICED
200G CARROTS, CLEANED AND FINELY SLICED
1 TEASPOON BLACK PEPPERCORNS
200ML DRY WHITE WINE
2 BAY LEAVES
A SMALL HANDFUL OF FRESH THYME
A SMALL BUNCH OF FLAT-LEAF PARSLEY
APPROX. 750ML WATER

A fabulous rice broth flavoured with saffron, the most expensive spice in the world (don't worry, we only use a pinch). Once the rice is ready this dish takes minutes.

mediterranean broth *with clams*

Pour the fish stock into a large saucepan and add the clams, courgettes, saffron and paprika. Simmer for 5 minutes, until the clams are open and then stir in the rice and crème fraîche.

Serve in bowls and top with whole fresh basil leaves (pictured opposite).

serves 4

PER SERVING 359 KCALS, PROTEIN 26G, CARBS 30.9G, FAT 13.4G, SAT FAT 7.3G, FIBRE 1.8G, SUGAR 3.2G, SALT 0.3G

600ML MEDITERRANEAN FISH STOCK (SEE PAGE 84)
650G LIVE CLAMS, CLEANED AND CHECKED (DISCARD
    ANY THAT DO NOT CLOSE OR HAVE BROKEN SHELLS)
200G COURGETTES, SLICED
A PINCH OF SAFFRON
1 TEASPOON SMOKED PAPRIKA
300G COOKED SHORTGRAIN WHITE RICE
100ML CRÈME FRAÎCHE (OPTIONAL)
LOTS OF BASIL LEAVES (USE LARGE AND SMALL)

Mackerel needs to be gutted and chilled on ice immediately after it is caught to keep the flesh firm and flavoursome. For this reason I rarely buy mackerel: fishermen consider it a cheap fish and don't give it the respect it needs. If you do manage to hustle a fine mackerel, please make this dish – it will make you feel good! I have cooked this using both fish and chicken stock, basing my decision on what I have in the fridge. Use fresh or dried seaweed, but remember that the dried version expands an awful lot on contact with water – about ten times!

mackerel *with brown rice noodles*

Heat the stock in a medium saucepan with the ginger. Once it reaches boiling point add the spinach and sea lettuce. Remove from the heat.

Meanwhile, heat a medium, non-stick frying pan and pour in a few drops of vegetable oil, just enough to line the base of the pan.

Coat the mackerel fillets in teriyaki sauce and sesame seeds. Fry over a moderate heat, skin side down, for 4 minutes. Turn and immediately remove from the heat or the fillets will become overcooked.

Cook the rice noodles in plenty of boiling water following the packet instructions.

Serve the broth poured on hot noodles topped with mackerel fillets and a few thin slices of red onion.

serves 2

PER SERVING 591 KCALS, PROTEIN 43.9G, CARBS 20G, FAT 33.9G, SAT FAT 6.7G, FIBRE 8.8G, SUGAR 5.9G, SALT 1.3G

500ML WHITE FISH STOCK OR CHICKEN STOCK
    (SEE PAGES 85 AND 52)
2CM PIECE (APPROX. 25G) GINGER, PEELED AND
    SLICED INTO MATCHSTICKS
APPROX. 100G WASHED BABY SPINACH LEAVES
50G PREPARED SEA LETTUCE, WASHED THREE TIMES TO
    REMOVE SALT AND SAND (IF YOU CAN'T FIND SEA
    LETTUCE USE ANY OTHER SEAWEED YOU FANCY)
VEGETABLE OIL
4 MACKEREL FILLETS
TERIYAKI SAUCE
SESAME SEEDS
200G BROWN RICE NOODLES
A FEW THIN SLICES OF RED ONION

I visited Copenhagen's Torvehallerne market recently, a mecca for serious foodies. The longest queue was at a cooked fish trader called Hav2Go. *Hav* means sea. Get it? Anyway, their fish frikadellers are seriously good served with turmeric mayo and pickled turnip. I've lightened up the recipe, removed the wheat and replaced it with ground almonds. The frikadellers are good hot or cold so if you have any left over try in a sandwich or salad.

frickin' frikadellic fish broth

Put the diced potatoes into a pan of boiling water and cook for 15 minutes until soft. Drain and allow to cool.

Simmer the fish stock, sliced turnip and leek for 10–12 minutes until the turnip is soft. Once it is cooked remove from the heat and stir in the coconut cream.

Meanwhile, mix together the frikadeller ingredients in a medium bowl – that's the fish, egg yolks, cooked potato, salt and white pepper and parsley. Roughly mash with a fork.

Spread out a couple of tablespoons of ground almonds onto a chopping board and, using the same tablespoon, fish out golf-ball sized portions of frikadeller mix, mould into discs and press into the ground almonds until coated. Use more almonds until you have coated all the frikadellers – you should end up with about 10.

Cover the base of a medium frying pan with oil and fry the frikadellers over a medium heat for 3 minutes on each side until golden brown.

Serve the broth in bowls, place a few frikadellers on top and sprinkle with toasted caraway seeds and sprigs of chervil.

serves 2

PER SERVING 677 KCALS, PROTEIN 29.4G, CARBS 32.2G, FAT 44.1G, SAT FAT 25.1G, FIBRE 10.3G, SUGAR 14.8, SALT 1G

500ML WHITE FISH STOCK (SEE PAGE 85)
250G TURNIPS, PEELED AND THINLY SLICED
150G LEEKS, WASHED AND SLICED
150ML COCONUT CREAM

FOR THE FRIKADELLERS
200G FLOURY POTATOES (NOT NEW POTATOES), PEELED AND DICED
150G WHITE FISH FILLET, ROUGHLY CHOPPED (I LIKE LEMON SOLE BUT USE ANY WHITE FISH YOU LIKE)
2 EGG YOLKS
SALT AND ¼ TEASPOON WHITE PEPPER
A SMALL BUNCH OF FLAT-LEAF PARSLEY, CHOPPED
GROUND ALMONDS, FOR COATING
VEGETABLE OIL, FOR FRYING

TO SERVE
1 TEASPOON CARAWAY SEEDS, DRY-FRIED OVER MEDIUM HEAT FOR 2 MINUTES
SPRIGS OF CHERVIL

I consider myself very lucky. I have two very good farmers' markets on my doorstep and I can usually find what I am after, including plantain and okra for this broth.

This year I travelled to Xcalak, on the Caribbean coast of Mexico near the border with Belize, and met Lupita, a clever, talented girl from a poor family. The one thing she did have was residual wifi from a holiday villa so I left her my tablet and she now Skypes my daughter in the UK – they're both eleven. Lupita took Amy on a virtual tour of her smallholding to reveal a scrawny flock of ducks, withered maize and a bubbling cauldron of fish stew, made from fish freshly speared by her father that morning, with the addition of rice, sweet potato, tomatoes and thyme. Their favourite fish for the stew is snapper or barracuda.

I recommend using a clear, nutritious classic fish stock for this recipe.

caribbean fish broth

Pour the fish stock into a large saucepan, add the plantain, okra, sweet potato, potato, tomatoes, carrots, onion and chilli and simmer for 30 minutes until all the vegetables are soft.

Add the fish fillets, thyme and lime juice. Season with salt and simmer for a further few minutes until the fish is just cooked.

Meanwhile blend the coriander, garlic and coconut cream into a paste.

Serve the fish broth topped with a generous spoonful of coriander paste.

serves 4

PER SERVING 340 KCALS, PROTEIN 30.3G, CARBS 31.2G, FAT 6.8G, SAT FAT 2.3G, FIBRE 8.9G, SUGAR 15.2G, SALT 0.4G

1.2 LITRES WHITE FISH STOCK (SEE PAGE 85)
1 GREEN PLANTAIN, PEELED AND SLICED
12 OKRA, TOPS REMOVED
1 MEDIUM SWEET POTATO, PEELED AND CUT INTO
   LARGE CHUNKS
1 MEDIUM POTATO, WASHED AND CUT INTO LARGE
   CHUNKS
3 MEDIUM TOMATOES, SLICED
2 CARROTS, PEELED AND ROUGHLY DICED
1 ONION, PEELED AND ROUGHLY DICED
1 HOT RED CHILLI
4 RED SNAPPER FILLETS OR 4 SEA BASS FILLETS
A COUPLE OF LARGE SPRIGS OF THYME
JUICE OF 1 LIME
SALT

FOR THE CORIANDER PASTE
A SMALL BUNCH OF CORIANDER
2 CLOVES GARLIC, CHOPPED
1 TABLESPOON COCONUT CREAM

Residents of Ancona turn away. I'm about to manipulate the famous Italian fish stew into something equally delicious, yet more accessible, dedicated to those who have an aversion to fish bones. The recipe from Ancona in the Marche province uses whole fish, including grey mantis shrimp and the famous Scorpion fish, from which you have to remove the sting before you add it to the pot! I'm happy to report that many other easily available varieties of fish and seafood are perfect for brodetto, including monkfish, seabass, squid, John Dory, whiting, hake, clam and langoustine.

My Mediterranean fish stock makes a perfect base and, if you've been organised and made it in advance, this recipe shouldn't take more than half an hour all in.

brodetto

To make the brodetto, pour the stock into a large saucepan, add the pepper, carrots, wine and balsamic vinegar and simmer for 20 minutes until the vegetables are soft. Add the oregano, thyme and all the fish fillets. Simmer for 5 minutes.

Add the squid and clams, cover the pan with the lid and simmer for a further 5 minutes until the clams are open.

Toss in the parsley and a generous glug of extra virgin olive oil, and season with salt and pepper.

While the brodetto cooks, empty the polenta and vegetable stock into a separate saucepan, bring to the boil and turn the heat down to low. Simmer away, stirring frequently until the polenta thickens to a porridgy consistency. Season with olive oil, salt and pepper.

Ladle portions of polenta into large soup bowls, followed by a generous serving of brodetto.

serves 2

PER SERVING 432 KCALS, PROTEIN 43.5G, CARBS 35.5G, FAT 8.5G, SAT FAT 1.1G, FIBRE 6.9G, SUGAR 10.4G, SALT 1G

1 LITRE MEDITERRANEAN FISH STOCK (SEE PAGE 84)
1 RED PEPPER, DICED
2 CARROTS, PEELED AND DICED
100ML DRY WHITE WINE
2 TABLESPOONS BALSAMIC VINEGAR
A SPRIG OR TWO OF OREGANO, CHOPPED
2 TEASPOONS CHOPPED FRESH THYME
600G (APPROX.) FISH FILLETS (ALL WHITE FISH – A
    GOOD COMBINATION WOULD BE: 200G
    MONKFISH FILLETS, CUT INTO LARGE CHUNKS,
    200G SEABASS FILLETS, 200G HAKE FILLETS)
1 SMALL SQUID, CLEANED AND SLICED
200G LIVE CLAMS, CLEANED AND CHECKED (DISCARD
    ANY THAT DO NOT CLOSE OR HAVE BROKEN
    SHELLS)
A SMALL BUNCH OF FLAT-LEAF PARSLEY, CHOPPED
EXTRA VIRGIN OLIVE OIL
SALT AND FRESHLY GROUND BLACK PEPPER

FOR THE POLENTA
120G COARSE POLENTA (I USE ORGANIC)
700ML VEGETABLE STOCK (SEE PAGE 100) OR WATER

Picture this. You return home, slightly depressed as the day didn't go quite as you would have liked. You lugubriously peer into the fridge and find, to your surprise, the Mediterranean fish stock you judiciously made at the weekend. A recipe is born and you feel much, much better! This is a dish of great flavour and beauty, created in minutes, and perfect for a mid-week meal.

fish broth
with prawns, herbs and fettuccini

Heat the fish stock in a medium saucepan and add the peppers and pasta. As soon as the stock boils remove from the heat and set aside until you need it.

Meanwhile, heat the olive oil in a frying pan over a medium heat until it is shimmering. Season the prawns with half the parsley, the lemon, paprika, garlic and salt. Fry over quite a fierce heat, constantly tossing for 3-4 minutes.

Stir the remaining parsley and the basil into the broth and pour into two bowls. Top with the cooked prawns.

serves 4
PER SERVING 533 KCALS, PROTEIN 58G, CARBS 39.1G, FAT 13.3G, SAT FAT 2G, FIBRE 6.4G, SUGAR 7.2G, SALT 3G

500ML MEDITERRANEAN FISH STOCK (SEE PAGE 84)
100G PIQUILLO PEPPERS, SLICED (SPANISH PRESERVED PEPPERS THAT ARE THIN-SKINNED AND DEEPLY FLAVOURED, AVAILABLE FROM MEDITERRANEAN DELIS AND SUPERMARKETS. IF YOU CAN'T FIND THEM USE REGULAR ROASTED PEPPERS FROM A JAR)
200G COOKED FETTUCCINI PASTA (80G WHEN DRY), OR SLIGHTLY MORE IF YOU'RE HUNGRY
1 TABLESPOON OLIVE OIL
10 MEDIUM RAW PRAWNS, EITHER PEELED OR SHELL ON
A SMALL BUNCH OF FLAT-LEAF PARSLEY, ROUGHLY CHOPPED
JUICE OF ½ LEMON
½ TEASPOON PAPRIKA OR SMOKED PAPRIKA
2 CLOVES GARLIC, FINELY CHOPPED
SALT
A SMALL BUNCH OF BASIL, LEAVES REMOVED AND ROUGHLY CHOPPED

Some sources say that this Flemish soup was originally made with burbot, a freshwater fish closely resembling cod. Sadly, these fish are practically extinct, so we'll make do with sustainable Alaskan salmon and mussels. This traditional broth is delicious made with chicken or chicken and pork stock, thickened with egg yolk and crème fraîche and served with fine French beans, potatoes and herbs.

waterzooi

Put the stock and white wine into a large saucepan with the new potatoes, swede, carrots and leek and simmer for 15 minutes until cooked.

Add the mussels, cover the pan with the lid and simmer for a further 5 minutes until the mussels have opened.

Remove from the heat and swirl in the egg yolks, mustard and crème fraîche.

Season the salmon fillets with salt and pepper and a scattering of caraway seeds. Pour a thin layer of olive oil into a frying pan over a medium heat. Fry the salmon for about 3 minutes on each side until just cooked.

Meanwhile, drop the French beans into a pan of boiling water and cook for 3 minutes until al dente. Drain, then toss them with a knob of butter and the garlic.

Serve the Waterzooi in bowls topped with the beans, salmon and sprigs of dill.

serves 4

PER SERVING 494 KCALS, PROTEIN 29.8G, CARBS 20.7G, FAT 29.1G, SAT FAT 10.6G, FIBRE 7.2G, SUGAR 10.3G, SALT 1.7G

600ML CHICKEN STOCK (SEE PAGE 52)
100ML DRY WHITE WINE, IDEALLY RIESLING
250G NEW POTATOES, SCRUBBED AND DICED
200G SWEDE, PEELED AND DICED
2 MEDIUM CARROTS, PEELED AND DICED
1 MEDIUM LEEK, WASHED AND DICED
24 MUSSELS, SCRUBBED CLEAN WITH NO KNOBBLY
    BITS OR BEARDS (DISCARD ANY THAT DO NOT
    CLOSE OR HAVE BROKEN SHELLS)
2 EGG YOLKS, LIGHTLY BEATEN
1 TEASPOON DIJON MUSTARD
100ML CRÈME FRAÎCHE
4 SKINLESS SALMON FILLETS (EACH APPROX. 100G)
SALT AND FRESHLY GROUND BLACK PEPPER
CARAWAY SEEDS
OLIVE OIL, FOR FRYING
300G FRENCH BEANS
KNOB OF BUTTER
1 CLOVE GARLIC, FINELY CHOPPED
A FEW SPRIGS OF DILL, TO SERVE

In Burma there's a fish called snakehead. It does all the things fish aren't supposed to do like survive on dry land, migrate from lake to lake and look after its babies. I've caught snakehead in a jungle clearing far from civilisation. They are never particularly happy to see you and as they snap their jaws together you need to steer clear of their razor-sharp teeth. The fact is, snakehead tastes delicious so the locals cook it up in their national dish. Sea bass are far less dangerous but equally delightful so that's what I've used in this recipe.

mohinga

Dry-fry the rice in a frying pan over a medium heat for 5 minutes until tanned. Make sure you constantly stir the rice as it browns. Crush the rice using a rolling pin, pestle and mortar or in a spice blender until the grains are granular but not powdered.

Heat 2 tablespoons of vegetable oil in a large saucepan over a lowish heat and gently fry the turmeric, ginger, lemongrass, shallot, chilli, shrimp paste, lime and garlic for 10 minutes, stirring frequently.

Add the fish stock and crushed rice. Bring to the boil and simmer for 20 minutes. If the stock reduces by more than 1cm, top up with a splash of hot water or more fish stock. The stock will become thick and slightly porridge-like towards the end of the cooking. At this point throw in the beans, simmer for a couple of minutes and then add the noodles and coconut cream.

Coat the sea bass with the fish sauce and dip in either polenta or semolina. Heat 1 tablespoon of vegetable oil in a frying pan over a medium heat, and fry the sea bass, skin-side down, for 4 minutes, then turn and fry for 2 minutes on the other side until the skin is crispy and the fish is cooked through.

Serve the broth immediately, topped with the crispy fish.

serves 4

PER SERVING 521 KCALS, PROTEIN 39.8G, CARBS 32.8G, FAT 25G, SAT FAT 9.6G, FIBRE 2.9G, SUGAR 5.4G, SALT 1.5G

1 HEAPED TABLESPOON JASMINE RICE
VEGETABLE OIL
1CM PIECE (APPROX. 10G) OF FRESH TURMERIC ROOT, FINELY CHOPPED
2CM PIECE (APPROX. 20G) OF FRESH GINGER ROOT, FINELY CHOPPED
½ LEMONGRASS STALK, FINELY CHOPPED
1 BANANA SHALLOT, FINELY CHOPPED
1 MEDIUM RED CHILLI, FINELY CHOPPED
10G BELACHAN (FERMENTED SHRIMP PASTE)
½ LIME, SKIN AND ALL, FINELY CHOPPED
2 CLOVES GARLIC, FINELY CHOPPED
500ML WHITE FISH STOCK (SEE PAGE 85)
10 RUNNER BEANS OR STRINGLESS FLAT BEANS, CUT INTO THIN STRIPS
200G COOKED FLAT RICE NOODLES
50G COCONUT CREAM

2 MEDIUM SEA BASS FILLETS
2 TEASPOONS FISH SAUCE
1 TABLESPOON POLENTA OR SEMOLINA

Vegetables

Even the most fanatical bone broth maker will run dry from time to time. On such occasions it's best to turn to the garden for inspiration. My veggie broth is both delicious and functional with the immune support of shiitake mushrooms and the anti-inflammatory properties of turmeric.

I use lovage in my veggie stock, a popular herb in mainland Europe, but it can be difficult to find, so don't worry if it's missing. If you do manage to unearth it don't use more than the stated amount in the recipe or its pungency will overpower the other ingredients.

One of the great beauties of making your own vegetable stock is that you are able to control the amount of salt. Mass market vegetable bouillons can contain up to 50% salt; the flavour in this stock is the essence of freshly chopped and simmered vegetables.

Old herbs and vegetables don't work in these stocks. Make sure your mushrooms are firm and that your herbs are deep green – ideally the ingredients should be organic. Stick to these rules and you'll luxuriate in veggie goodness.

My veggie stock is light and fragrant – great for seasonal garden broths. If you can't find the lovage or fresh turmeric don't worry, just leave them out!

vegetable stock

Place all ingredients, apart from the water, in a bowl chopper and pulse until finely chopped.

Turn out into a large saucepan, followed by the boiling water from the kettle.

Bring to the boil and simmer for 15 minutes, then pass through a conical sieve, if you have one, or just use a strainer. Make sure you press the cooked vegetables down using the back of a large spoon to obtain the maximum amount of stock.

makes 1.5 litres

PER 100G 16 KCALS, PROTEIN 0.8G, CARBS 2.2G, FAT 0.2G, SAT FAT 0G, FIBRE 1G, SUGAR 1G, SALT 0.3G

2 FRESH BAY LEAVES
2G FRESH ROSEMARY
40G BROWN MUSHROOMS
100G BUTTERNUT SQUASH, ROUGHLY CHOPPED
50G SHIITAKE MUSHROOMS
1 TEASPOON FENNEL SEEDS
80G FRESH FLAT-LEAF PARSLEY
80G CELERY STICK
4G FRESH LOVAGE LEAVES (OPTIONAL)
150G CARROTS, WASHED, TRIMMED
100G SHALLOTS
10G OR 1 LARGE CLOVE GARLIC
100G LEEKS, WASHED
2 PIECES (APPROX. 25G) OF FRESH TURMERIC ROOT, WASHED
2 TEASPOONS SALT
½ TEASPOON GROUND WHITE PEPPER
1.25 LITRES BOILING WATER, STRAIGHT FROM THE KETTLE

A light veggie meal for two, prepared with seasonal vegetables and delicately scented edible flowers. Perfect for lunch.

light risotto broth
with spring veg and flowers

Heat the stock and add the butternut squash and courgette. Simmer for 5–7 minutes until soft.

Add the broccoli, rice and greens. Simmer for a further couple of minutes but don't boil. Season with salt, if needed.

Serve in large bowls garnished with edible flowers.

serves 4
PER SERVING 202 KCALS, PROTEIN 7.5G, CARBS 34.8G, FAT 2.2G, SAT FAT 0.4G, FIBRE 6.7G, SUGAR 7.3G, SALT 0.8G

600ML HOMEMADE VEGETABLE STOCK
   (SEE PAGE 100)
100G BUTTERNUT SQUASH, PEELED
   AND CUT INTO SMALL CUBES
100G COURGETTE, DICED
50G TINY FLORETS OF BROCCOLI
150G COOKED SHORTGRAIN WHITE RISOTTO RICE
50G SHREDDED GREENS OF YOUR CHOICE
A HANDFUL OF EDIBLE FLOWERS,
   SUCH AS BORAGE, GARLIC, VIOLET,
   MARIGOLD OR FENNEL, TO GARNISH
SALT

At the Medieval fair in Caminha, Portugal they take their *Caldo Verde* seriously. The literal translation is 'green broth' but the locals are quite particular about the ingredients. Kale, the defining frilly leaf, should be finely chopped. If you are using winter kale, which is more robust, you should simmer it for a minute or two longer. The potatoes have to be large, floury and thinly sliced so that they break up into small pieces imparting a slightly rough, granular feel on the tongue. Ours is a vegetarian version but in Caminha smoked sausage is served as an accompaniment. Instead, ours is topped with a smoky, herby pesto and roasted cherry tomatoes.

caldo verde

Preheat the oven to 180°C/160°C fan/gas mark 4.

Place the tomatoes, cut side up, on a baking tray and splash with a little olive oil and balsamic vinegar and roast for 30 minutes.

Meanwhile, heat a little olive oil in a large saucepan over a lowish heat and gently fry the red onion and garlic, stirring frequently until soft, for about 10 minutes.

Add the stock and potato. Simmer for 20–30 minutes, until the potato breaks up.

To make the pesto, Spread the walnuts on a second tray and dry-roast in the oven for 6 minutes until a shade darker. Remove and cool slightly.

Pulse the walnuts in the food processor until roughly chopped and tip into a small bowl. Stir in the basil, parsley, smoked paprika, salt, garlic, lemon juice and extra virgin olive oil.

Add the kale to the soup, simmer for a couple of minutes and serve in bowls topped with the pesto and roasted tomatoes.

serves 4

PER SERVING 353 KCALS, PROTEIN 11.5G, CARBS 32.1G, FAT 17.5G, SAT FAT 2.1G, FIBRE 10.8G, SUGAR 8.1G, SALT 1.5G

20 CHERRY TOMATOES, SLICED IN HALF
OLIVE OIL
BALSAMIC VINEGAR
1 RED ONION, FINELY DICED
4 CLOVES GARLIC, THINLY SLICED
1 LITRE VEGETABLE STOCK (SEE PAGE 100)
2 LARGE FLOURY POTATOES (APPROX. 500G), PEELED AND THINLY SLICED
400G KALE, THICK STALKS REMOVED, WASHED AND FINELY SHREDDED INTO MANAGEABLE SPOON-SIZE PIECES

FOR THE PESTO
50G SHELLED WALNUTS
A SMALL BUNCH OF BASIL, FINELY CHOPPED
A SMALL BUNCH OF FLAT-LEAF PARSLEY, FINELY CHOPPED
½ TEASPOON SMOKED PAPRIKA
½ TEASPOON SALT
½ CLOVE GARLIC, FINELY CHOPPED
JUICE OF ½ LEMON
A TABLESPOON OF EXTRA VIRGIN OLIVE OIL

I love this exotically flavoured North African broth with roasted cauliflower and the gentle spice of *ras el hanout*. The original recipe for this exotic seasoning was said to contain up to 50 spices including saffron and rose petals. Your shop-bought version may have skimped on the saffron, and swapped it for turmeric, but it will likely contain warming cardamom, cinnamon, nutmeg, cloves, cumin, ginger and coriander.

turmeric cauliflower and roasted corn

Preheat the oven to 200°C/180°C fan/gas mark 6.

Carefully mix the cauliflower with the turmeric, 1 tablespoon of olive oil and some salt. Spread the florets on a small baking tray. Coat the butternut squash with olive oil and spread the pieces on a second baking tray. Bake the cauliflower for 15 minutes and the squash for a little longer, about 20.

Meanwhile, heat a little oil in a large saucepan over a medium heat and fry the corn kernels until slightly charred. Remove the kernels, add 1 tablespoon of oil to the pan and gently fry the onion, garlic and *ras el hanout* for 10 minutes, stirring frequently.

Add the vegetable stock, ground almonds, corn, diced tomatoes and tomato purée. Simmer for 15 minutes.

When the vegetables have roasted, remove the trays from the oven and lower the temperature to 180°C/160°C fan/gas mark 4. Spread the flaked almonds in a small baking tray and bake for 6 minutes. Watch them carefully as they burn easily.

Stir the cauliflower and butternut squash into the broth, bring to the boil and season with salt.

Serve topped with the flaked almonds.

serves 2

PER SERVING 461 KCALS, PROTEIN 19.3G, CARBS 34.9G, FAT 23.7G, SAT FAT 3.2G, FIBRE 15.4G, SUGAR 22.4G, SALT 1.1G

1 MEDIUM CAULIFLOWER, DIVIDED INTO FLORETS
2 TEASPOONS TURMERIC
OLIVE OIL
SALT
½ SMALL BUTTERNUT SQUASH, PEELED AND DICED INTO 2CM CHUNKS
1 CORN ON THE COB, KERNELS SHAVED OFF COB WITH A SHARP KNIFE
1 MEDIUM ONION, FINELY CHOPPED
2 CLOVES GARLIC, FINELY CHOPPED
2 TEASPOONS *RAS EL HANOUT*
500ML VEGETABLE STOCK (SEE PAGE 100)
2 TABLESPOONS GROUND ALMONDS
4 TOMATOES, DICED
1 TABLESPOON OF TOMATO PURÉE
2 TABLESPOONS FLAKED ALMONDS

This broth is perfect at the beginning of the season when the peas and broad beans are small and juicy. I recommend this dish as a light lunch as it doesn't sit heavily in the tummy. Remember, the vegetable stock base can be made in advance, as can the almond cream and polenta, so with a bit of forward planning this dish can be constructed in minutes.

Making almond cream is a joyful and cathartic experience. Who would think that a small pile of blanched almonds soaked in water would produce such a light cream, perfect as a dairy substitute?

Polenta is not tricky to make but you do have to stand over it, constantly stirring the granular mix to stop it sticking to the base of the saucepan. If you really have to perform another task in the kitchen or elsewhere I'd take the polenta off the heat until you're ready to agitate, but don't wait too long as it solidifies readily!

broad beans, peas and polenta

Line a non-stick shallow baking tray with greaseproof paper.

Put the polenta, stock or water, chilli, porcini powder (if using), olive oil and a pinch of salt into a saucepan, bring to the boil and turn the heat down to low. Simmer away, stirring frequently until the polenta thickens into a porridgy consistency. Pour the polenta into the lined tray and level the surface. Set aside to cool.

Preheat the oven to 220°C/200° fan/gas mark 7.

Top the polenta with grated Parmesan, if using, and bake in the oven for 15 minutes. Remove and cut into squares. The polenta can be made in advance and kept in the fridge for up to 3 days.

To make the almond cream, soak the almonds in water for at least 6 hours, preferably overnight. Drain, then blend the almonds with 200ml water in a food processor for at least 1 minute until you have a juicy paste.

Squeeze the cream out through a fine sieve, muslin or cheesecloth. You should end up with about 120ml of almond cream. Compost the remaining pulp – a bit wasteful I know, but it's worth it! The almond cream can be made in advance and kept in the fridge for couple of days.

When you are ready to serve, heat the stock in a large saucepan over a medium heat, and simmer the peas and broad beans in the hot stock for a minute or two. Stir in the almond milk and parsley and season, if you like, with salt and pepper.

Serve in bowls, topped with the polenta and tarragon sprigs.

serves 2

PER SERVING 641 KCALS, PROTEIN 19.7G, CARBS 62.8G, FAT 31.2G, SAT FAT 4.2G, FIBRE 14.9G, SUGAR 6.8G, SALT 3.5G

FOR THE POLENTA
120G COARSE POLENTA (I USE ORGANIC)
700ML VEGETABLE STOCK (SEE PAGE 100) OR WATER
A PINCH OF FLAKED CHILLI, SMOKED OR UNSMOKED
½ TEASPOON PORCINI POWDER (OPTIONAL)
50ML OLIVE OIL
SALT
30–50G PARMESAN (OPTIONAL), GRATED

FOR THE ALMOND CREAM
150G BLANCHED ALMONDS

FOR THE BROTH
400ML VEGETABLE STOCK (SEE PAGE 100)
150G SHELLED BABY PEAS
150G SHELLED BROAD BEANS
A SMALL BUNCH OF FLAT-LEAF PARSLEY, ROUGHLY CHOPPED
SALT AND FRESHLY GROUND BLACK PEPPER
2–3 SPRIGS OF TARRAGON

A couple of years ago, before the spiraliser had been invented, all vegetables were straight. Now they're curvy and the world is a much better place. (I bought myself a fringed wig and a spiraliser on the same memorable day and have taken great pleasure from both.) Curled vegetables are texturally inviting and provide a great carb-free alternative to spaghetti. Kids love them (especially deep fried) and they're fab in broths. So get your spiraliser out and create this tasty broth. The pesto can be made in advance and will keep in the fridge in an airtight container for up to a week. And make sure you wear the wig!

spiralised veg and black rice noodles
with kale pesto

Toast the hazelnuts in a dry frying pan over a medium heat for 5 minutes, tossing occasionally. Tip out of the pan and allow to cool.

Roughly blend the pesto ingredients in the food processor. The pesto is best when granular, not smooth.

Spiralise the vegetables. Heat the stock in a large saucepan and briefly simmer the vegetables and noodles in the hot stock.

Serve in bowls topped with the pesto.

serves 2

PER SERVING 444 KCALS, PROTEIN 11.8G, CARBS 26G, FAT 30.2G, SAT FAT 3.7G, FIBRE 10.5G, SUGAR 9.4G, SALT 2.4G

YOU WILL NEED A SPIRALISER

FOR THE PESTO
25G BLANCHED HAZELNUTS
A SMALL BUNCH OF FLAT-LEAF PARSLEY
50G KALE
40ML OLIVE OIL
½ TEASPOON SALT
1 CLOVE GARLIC, ROUGHLY CHOPPED
1 SMALL GREEN CHILLI, ROUGHLY CHOPPED

1 LARGE CARROT, PEELED
1 MEDIUM COURGETTE
1 BROCCOLI STALK (APPROX. 100G)
600ML VEGETABLE OR CHICKEN STOCK (SEE PAGES 100 AND 52)
200G COOKED BLACK RICE NOODLES (OR, IF YOU CAN'T FIND THESE, ANY NOODLES WILL DO!)

This is the only broth recipe in the book where the vegetables are fried prior to adding the stock. I hope you don't think any worse of me. I know that I'm swerving towards soup, but caramelising the shallots makes them sweet and soft, perfect with pomegranate molasses, fresh chopped tomatoes and toasted spice. That's my excuse!

Harira
with Saffron & Freekeh

Dry fry the nigella, cumin and mustard seeds in a medium size saucepan for a few minutes, stirring frequently until the mustard seeds start popping.

Add the olive oil, garlic and shallots. Gently fry, stirring occasionally until the shallots are soft, about 10 minutes

Add the tomatoes and continue to simmer until the mixture becomes mushy. Add the pomegranate molasses, stock and saffron and simmer for 15-20 minutes.

Finally, add the freekeh and serve.

serves 4

PER SERVING 179 KCALS, PROTEIN 7.8G, CARBS 24.4G, FAT 4.2G, SAT FAT 0.5G, FIBRE 6G, SUGAR 8.8G, SALT 0.4G

1 TEASPOON NIGELLA SEEDS
1 TEASPOON CUMIN SEEDS
1 TEASPOON MUSTARD SEEDS
1 TABLESPOON OLIVE OIL
2 CLOVES GARLIC, CHOPPED
250G SHALLOTS, PEELED AND SLICED
300G TOMATOES, CHOPPED
2 TEASPOONS POMEGRANATE MOLASSES
500ML VEGETABLE STOCK OR CHICKEN STOCK (SEE PAGES 100 AND 52)
A PINCH OF SAFFRON
200G COOKED FREEKEH (80-90G UNCOOKED)

'We should breathe in love and breathe out kindness' was my wife's unexpected comment after a yoga retreat in Lesbos. And she did exactly that for months afterwards (with a couple of temporary aberrations). I dedicate this dish to those who have had a change of heart. Yes, it's worthy and a bit of a weird combination, but it works! Seek out a good mango before you cook up this broth – sweet, golden and juicy!

avocado, cashews and roasted corn

Preheat the oven to 220°C/200°C fan/gas mark 7.

Bake the corn on the cob for 30 minutes until golden brown. (Alternatively, if you have a barbecue, cook them until charred on all sides.) Remove and allow to cool. Once you can touch the corn without burning your fingers run a knife down each cob to remove the individual kernels.

Lower the oven temperature to 180°C/160°C fan/gas mark 4. Spread out the cashew nuts in a small baking tray and roast for 8 minutes until golden brown.

To make the dressing, blend the soaked and drained cashew nuts, tahini, almond milk, teriyaki sauce, ginger, chilli and rice vinegar in a food processor until smooth.

Heat the stock in a large saucepan and add the corn, avocado, mango, greens and lime juice.

Serve in bowls with a very large tablespoon of cashew dressing on top and a pile of cashews.

serves 4

PER SERVING 639 KCALS, PROTEIN 18.9G, CARBS 23.6G, FAT 49.5G, SAT FAT 9.3G, FIBRE 11.7G, SUGAR 8.2G, SALT 0.9G

2 CORN ON THE COB
100G CASHEW NUTS
500ML VEGETABLE OR CHICKEN STOCK (SEE PAGES 100 AND 52)
1 AVOCADO, PEELED, STONED AND DICED
1 MANGO, PEELED, STONED AND DICED
50G LEAFY GREENS, SHREDDED
JUICE OF 1 LIME

FOR THE CASHEW DRESSING
70G CASHEW NUTS, SOAKED IN WATER FOR AT LEAST 6 HOURS, PREFERABLY OVERNIGHT, PLUS EXTRA TO SERVE
100G TAHINI
100ML UNSWEETENED ALMOND MILK
20ML TERIYAKI SAUCE
2CM PIECE (APPROX. 15G) OF FRESH GINGER ROOT, SLICED
1 HOT GREEN CHILLI, SLICED
20ML RICE VINEGAR

steamboats

Steamboats are fondues without cheese and without the guilt associated with consuming one's annual allowance of saturated fat in a single meal. Steamboats are as versatile as they are fun; they are healthy and great to share with friends. The recipes that follow are starter kits, just enough to give you a base from which you can flourish. Experiment with thin slices of meat, greens, noodles and dumplings.

Steamboats come in all sorts of shapes and sizes. The one in the book uses glowing charcoal to heat the broth and there is also an electric version. I once created a seafood steamboat while cruising around the Mentawi Islands of Indonesia using a camp stove and a battered metal bowl. That was the first and last time I had a steamboat on a boat! You could improvise with a wok set over a portable gas burner but it's safest to buy a steamboat from an Asian supermarket.

According to my wife, the Goddess of Mercy lives on the moon with a giant rabbit. Every autumn we celebrate the harvest moon with a family steamboat – an event not to be missed!

I start my steamboats with a 50:50 mix of chicken stock to water. You will need to alter volumes according to the size of your steamboat but aim to fill it at least halfway. Make sure you have chopsticks, wire spoons and tongs to retrieve those slippery wontons and, once the stock is simmering, you're ready to start.

chinese steamboat

Put the chilli, ginger, garlic, fish and fish sauce in a food processor and pulse until sticky but not smooth.

Throw in the coriander and continue to pulse in little bursts until loosely stuck together.

Form into chicken nugget-sized balls or, if you've never eaten a chicken nugget, smaller than golf balls, larger than marbles! You should make about 12. Dampen your hands so that the mix doesn't stick to your fingers. Store in an airtight container in the fridge until you need them.

Mix the minced pork, chilli, garlic, ginger, spring onions, fish sauce and sesame oil using your fingers until sticky.

Lay out a wonton wrapper and paint with a thin layer of egg wash. Pick up a small pile of minced pork with a teaspoon and place in the centre of the wonton wrapper. Pull up the corners and squeeze together. Repeat with the remaining mince – you should make 20–24 wontons. Store in an airtight container in the fridge until you need them.

Gently heat your stock in the steamboat until simmering. Assemble all your dipping ingredients. The fishballs and wontons will need to simmer in the stock for at least 8 minutes but the broccoli and mushrooms won't take long at all and the chillis take seconds. Merely dip the vermicelli in and it will heat up immediately.

Feel free to embellish your steamboat with any other meat or veg that you fancy but make sure you cook chicken and pork thoroughly.

serves 4

PER SERVING 656 KCALS, PROTEIN 51.1G, CARBS 39.4G, FAT 32.1G, SAT FAT 3.9G, FIBRE 2.7G, SUGAR 3.6G, SALT 3.3G

FOR 4 PEOPLE YOU WILL NEED A 26–28CM STEAMBOAT

FOR THE FISHBALLS
1 RED CHILLI, ROUGHLY SLICED
2CM PIECE (APPROX. 15G) OF FRESH GINGER ROOT, PEELED AND ROUGHLY SLICED
2 CLOVES GARLIC, ROUGHLY CHOPPED
200G FRESH WHITE FISH FILLET, CUT INTO SMALL CHUNKS
15ML FISH SAUCE
15G FRESH CORIANDER LEAVES

FOR THE WONTONS
250G ROUGHLY MINCED PORK
1 RED CHILLI, FINELY CHOPPED
1 CLOVE GARLIC, FINELY CHOPPED
1CM PIECE (APPROX. 10G) OF FRESH GINGER ROOT, FINELY CHOPPED
3 SPRING ONIONS, THINLY SLICED
15ML FISH SAUCE
15ML SESAME OIL
1 PACK OF WONTON WRAPPERS
1 SMALL EGG, LIGHTLY BEATEN

FOR THE STEAMBOAT
APPROX. 1 LITRE CHICKEN STOCK (SEE PAGE 52) PLUS 1 LITRE WATER, ENOUGH TO HALF FILL YOUR STEAMBOAT
LONG STEM BROCCOLI
SHIMEJI OR SHIITAKE MUSHROOMS
COOKED RICE VERMICELLI (SEE PAGE 13)
CHOPPED RED CHILLIES
SWEET CHILLI SAUCE, FOR DIPPING

I first tasted *Shabu Shabu* in Tokyo, where it's become quite a craze. Each table in the restaurant has its own steamboat, ready to go. Ingredients are ordered from an extensive menu, including marbled Wagyu beef, if you can afford it, and live shrimp – not for the squeamish. *Shabu Shabu* is onomatopoeic and, within seconds, as you swish your meat to and fro you find yourself uttering the smutty words 'sheeaabu sheeaabu' and smirking at fellow diners, who take no notice of you at all.

Shabu Shabu can be made with a base of dashi – that's bonito tuna and kombu seaweed stock – but I find it too delicate and prefer a more robust chicken and pork stock.

japanese shabu shabu

To make the gyoza, toast the sesame seeds in a dry frying pan over a medium heat for 3–4 minutes until golden. Tip into a small bowl and mix in the diced scallops, chives, sesame oil, ginger and teriyaki sauce.

Lay out a gyoza skin and paint with a thin layer of egg wash. Pick up a small pile of scallop mix with a teaspoon and place in the centre of the wrapper. Pull up the sides and squeeze together. Repeat with the remaining mixture – you should make about 20. Store in an airtight container in the fridge until you need them.

To prepare the pork belly, place in the freezer for 1 hour until half frozen. Then, using your sharpest knife, cut into ultra-thin slices – the thinner they are the more tender they will be. If you are not confident doing this, ask your butcher or a friend with a steady hand to do it.

Gently heat your stock in the steamboat until simmering. Assemble all your dipping ingredients. Take care with the pork belly as it needs 4–5 minutes to cook through. The rest of the ingredients should be cooked according to taste, although I would recommend cooking the gyoza for around 5 minutes.

serves 4

PER SERVING 624 KCALS, PROTEIN 48.8G, CARBS 33.7G, FAT 32G, SAT FAT 5.4G, FIBRE 2.8G, SUGAR 3.4G, SALT 2.8G

FOR THE GYOZA
1 TEASPOON SESAME SEEDS
6 SCALLOPS, CLEANED, REMOVED FROM THE SHELL AND FINELY DICED
20 CHIVES, CHOPPED
1 TEASPOON SESAME OIL
1CM PIECE (APPROX. 10G) OF FRESH GINGER ROOT, FINELY CHOPPED
2 TEASPOONS TERIYAKI SAUCE
1 PACK OF FRESH GYOZA SKINS (YOU CAN FREEZE ANY LEFT OVER)
1 SMALL EGG, LIGHTLY BEATEN

FOR THE STEAMBOAT
APPROX. 2 LITRES CHICKEN STOCK (SEE PAGE 52), ENOUGH TO HALF FILL YOUR STEAMBOAT
300G PORK BELLY, SKIN AND BONE REMOVED
8–12 LARGE PRAWNS
DRIED MIXED SEAWEED, SOAKED AND SQUEEZED OUT TO REMOVE SALT AND GRIT
COOKED SOBA NOODLES (SEE PAGE 13)
PONZU SAUCE, FOR DIPPING

If China, Japan and Korea can do it, why can't we? The best way to serve fine, fresh British ingredients is to briefly waft them in slow-cooked beef bone broth. And if wafting isn't your thing you can simmer your dumplings!

steamboat

with beef, horseradish dumplings and garden vegetables

Rub the suet into the flour, salt and baking powder in a large bowl. Add the horseradish and mustard powder. Gradually mix in water until the dough comes together but is firm.

Form into dumplings slightly smaller than table tennis balls using damp hands; otherwise they will stick to your fingers.

Gently heat your stock in the steamboat until simmering. Assemble all your dipping ingredients. The dumplings take 10-12 minutes and float when ready. The courgettes, turnips, carrots and salad onions will take 4-5 minutes to cook, whereas the sugarsnap peas will take just 30 seconds.

If you like your steak rare, swirl it around in the stock for 10-15 seconds before removing, otherwise keep it in for longer. After a minute it will be cooked through.

Other ingredients you could use are chestnut mushrooms, savoy cabbage, sliced Brussels sprouts and asparagus.

serves 4

PER SERVING 577 KCALS, PROTEIN 36.2G, CARBS 42.4G, FAT 27.5G, SAT FAT 13.9G, FIBRE 7.5G, SUGAR 8.5G, SALT 1G

FOR THE DUMPLINGS
120G SHREDDED SUET
250G PLAIN FLOUR
½ TEASPOON SALT
1 TEASPOON BAKING POWDER
40G FINELY GRATED FRESH HORSERADISH (TO AVOID TEARS GRATE IT WEARING SWIMMING GOGGLES OR WORK OUTSIDE)
1 TEASPOON MUSTARD POWDER

FOR THE STEAMBOAT
APPROX. 2 LITRES BEEF STOCK (SEE PAGE 17), ENOUGH TO HALF FILL YOUR STEAMBOAT
300G COURGETTES, SLICED IF LARGE
8 BABY TURNIPS, TRIMMED
12 BABY CARROTS
12 LARGE SALAD ONIONS
100G SUGARSNAP PEAS
400G RIBEYE STEAK, THINLY SLICED (IT IS SLIGHTLY EASIER TO SLICE IF YOU PARTIALLY FREEZE THE STEAK BEFOREHAND)
WORCESTERSHIRE SAUCE, FOR DIPPING

Index

Bibliography

FitzGibbon, Theodora **The Food of the Western World** (Random House Inc, 1976)

Drummond, J.C. and Wilbraham, Anne **The Englishman's Food: Five Centuries of English Diet** (Pimlico, 1994)

Renfrew, Jane **Prehistoric Cookery: Recipes and History** (London: English Heritage, 2005)

Mrs Beeton's **All About Cookery** (Ward, Lock, 1923)

Wilson, Bee **Swindled** (US: Princeton University Press, 2008)

Cobbett, William **Cottage Economy** (1826)

The State Chinese (Penang) Association **Nonya Flavours** (Malaysia: Star Publications, 2003)

Allen, Darina **Ballymaloe Cookery Course** (London: Kyle Books, 2013)

Lonely Planet **The World's Best Street Food** (Lonely PLanet, 2012)

Francatelli, Charles Elmé **A Plain Cookery Book for the Working Classes** (1852)

Costamagno S. **Bone grease rendering in Mousterian contexts: the case of Noisetier Cave** (France: Fre'chet-Aure, Hautes-Pyre'ne'es, 2013).

Longo V.D. et al. **A periodic diet that mimics fasting promotes multi-system regeneration, enhanced cognitive performance and healthspan.** Cell Metabolism, 22(1) (2015), 86-99.

Rennard B.O., Ertl R.F., Gossman G.L., Robbins R.A., Rennard S.I. **Chicken soup inhibits neutrophil chemotaxis in vitro.** Chest, 118 (2000), 1150-1157

Roberts S.J., Smith C.I., Millard A.R., Collins M.J. **The taphonomy of cooked bone: characterizing boiling and its physic-chemical effects.** Archaeometry, 44(3) (2002), 185-494.

Speth J.D. **When did humans learn to boil?** Paleo Anthropology, (2015), 54-67.

Spector T. **The Diet Myth: The Real Science Behind What We Eat.** (London: Weidenfeld & Nicolson, 2015)

Taubes G. **Why We Get Fat: And What To Do About It.** (US: Alfred A. Knopf, 2011)

Whiteman, Honor **"Fasting: health benefits and risks."** Medical News Today. MediLexicon, Intl., 27 Jul. 2015. Web.

Acknowledgements

I extend my heartfelt thanks to Linda Tubby and Ali Allen for interpreting my recipes beautifully over a short but intense period of photography. Mark Latter's stunning design has made this book incredibly attractive. Thanks to Ruth Ferrier for agreeing to draw the striking illustrations. And many thanks to Alina for her nutritional know-how.

It would be fair to say that my family have mostly ignored me in recent months, although they're always keen to taste new recipes. I'm really lucky that they take my moodiness with a pinch of salt and that they laughed when I inadvertently poured the stock down the plughole.

Lastly, thanks to Kyle for asking me to write this book and Claire, who's put it all together. It's been a joy!